Concurrent Crash-Prone Shared Memory Systems

A Few Theoretical Notions

Synthesis Lectures on Distributed Computing Theory

Editor
Michel Raynal, *University of Rennes, France and Hong Kong Polytechnic University*

Founding Editor
Nancy Lynch, *Massachusetts Institute of Technology*

Synthesis Lectures on Distributed Computing Theory was founded by Nancy Lynch of the Massachusetts Institute of Technology, and is now edited by Michel Raynal of the University of Rennes, France and Hong Kong Polytechnic University. The series publishes 50- to 150-page publications on topics pertaining to distributed computing theory. The scope largely follows the purview of premier information and computer science conferences, such as ACM PODC, DISC, SPAA, OPODIS, CONCUR, DialM-POMC, ICDCS, SODA, Sirocco, SSS, and related conferences. Potential topics include, but not are limited to: distributed algorithms and lower bounds, algorithm design methods, formal modeling and verification of distributed algorithms, and concurrent data structures.

Communication and Agreement Abstractions for Fault-Tolerant Asynchronous
Distributed Systems
Michel Raynal
2010

The Mobile Agent Rendezvous Problem in the Ring
Evangelos Kranakis, Danny Krizanc, and Euripides Markou
2010

Concurrent Crash-Prone Shared Memory Systems: A Few Theoretical Notions
Michel Raynal

ISBN: 978-3-031-79201-4   paperback
ISBN: 978-3-031-79213-7   PDF
ISBN: 978-3-031-79225-0   hardcover

DOI 10.1007/978-3-031-79213-7

A Publication in the Springer series
SYNTHESIS LECTURES ON DISTRIBUTED COMPUTING THEORY

Lecture #18
Series Editor: Michel Raynal, *University of Rennes, France and Hong Kong Polytechnic University*
Founding Editor: Nancy Lynch, *Massachusetts Institute of Technology*
Series ISSN
Print 2155-1626   Electronic 2155-1634

Concurrent Crash-Prone Shared Memory Systems

A Few Theoretical Notions

Michel Raynal

University of Rennes, France
Hong Kong Polytechnic University

SYNTHESIS LECTURES ON DISTRIBUTED COMPUTING THEORY #18

ABSTRACT

Theory is what remains true when technology is changing. So, it is important to know and master the basic concepts and the theoretical tools that underlie the design of the systems we are using today and the systems we will use tomorrow. This means that, given a computing model, we need to know what can be done and what cannot be done in that model. Considering systems built on top of an asynchronous read/write shared memory prone to process crashes, this monograph presents and develops the fundamental notions that are universal constructions, consensus numbers, distributed recursivity, power of the BG simulation, and what can be done when one has to cope with process anonymity and/or memory anonymity. Numerous distributed algorithms are presented, the aim of which is being to help the reader better understand the power and the subtleties of the notions that are presented. In addition, the reader can appreciate the simplicity and beauty of some of these algorithms.

KEYWORDS

abortable object, agreement, anonymous memory, anonymous process, asynchrony, atomic operation, bg simulation, branching time, concurrent object, consensus, consensus hierarchy, crash failure, deterministic object, distributed algorithm, distributed computability, distributed task, help mechanism, linear time, memory location, non-blocking, obstruction-freedom, progress condition, read/write register, recursion, reduction, renaming, shared memory, write-snapshot, sequential specification, k-set agreement, k-simultaneous consensus, speculative execution, universal construction, wait-freedom

To Jules, Aurore, and Quentin.

Contents

List of Figures

List of Algorithms

List of Tables

Preface

Teaching is not an accumulation of facts.
L. Lamport [95]

Correctness may be theoretical, ... but incorrectness has practical impact.
M. Herlihy

- Don't you have a more recent newspaper? I've known these news for two days.
- Read them again. In a few days they will be new again.
La Marca del Viento (2019), Eduardo Fernando Valera

Theory is what allows us to understand the deep nature of what we are doing. Technology is what should make our physical life more comfortable. With this spirit in mind, this book addresses five topics of the theory of distributed concurrent systems in which the computing entities (processes) are asynchronous (each proceeds at its own speed), can unexpectedly crash, and where communication is through atomic read/write registers. The topics addressed are the (i) notion of universal constructions, (ii) the notion of consensus numbers, (iii) the notion of distributed recursivity, (iv) the BG simulation, and (v) the notion of anonymity (anonymous processes and anonymous memory). Each of the five chapters is devoted to one of these topics.

For each topic the book presents associated concepts and mechanisms. Many algorithms are described to illustrate the notions that are developed. A few repetitions are done in order to allow each chapter to be read independently from the other chapters.

This book does not consider the case where the computing entities communicate through an underlying message-passing system. This type of communication is addressed in [116] for failure-free message-passing systems and in [120, 121] for failure-prone message-passing. The reader will also find in [136] a very nice introduction to what makes *distributed computing* one of the most challenging areas in Informatics for the 21st century. The reader interested in impossibility results in distributed computing will consult [11]. The reader interested in the *spirit* of algorithms will have a look at [65].

Tous les pays qui n'ont plus de légendes sont condamnés à mourir de froid.[1]
Patrice de la Tour du Pin (1911–1975)

Michel Raynal
February 2022

---

[1] All countries that no longer have legends will be condemned to die of cold.

Acknowledgments

I thank all the authors cited in the bibliography (... and many others whose articles have improved my knowledge and influenced my view of distributed computing). Without their works this book would not exist!

Special thanks to Carole Delporte, Hugues Fauconnier, Davide Frey, Antonio Fermandez Anta, Damien Imbs, Achour Mostéfaoui, Sergio Rajsbaum, François Taïani, and Gadi Taubenfeld with whom I have had many technical discussions on synchronization and concurrent systems, and more general discussions on the nature of Informatics and the essence of distributed computing.

Michel Raynal
(September–November 2021)
Saint-Grégoire, Saint-Philibert

CHAPTER 1

Distributed Universality

The notion of a universal construction is central in Informatics: the wheel has not to be reinvented for each new problem (as a trivial example, when we write a new program we do not need to design a new specific compiler to translate it in a given machine language). In the context of n-process asynchronous distributed systems, a universal construction is an algorithm that is able to build any object defined by a sequential specification despite the occurrence of up to $(n-1)$ process crash failures. The aim of this chapter is to present an introduction to such universal constructions. Its spirit is not to be a catalog of the numerous constructions proposed so far, but to be an as simple as possible presentation of the basic concepts and mechanisms that constitute the basis these constructions rest on.

Keywords: Abortable object, Agreement problem, Asynchronous read/write system, Atomic operations, Computability, Concurrent object, Consensus, Crash failure, Disjoint-access parallelism, Generalized universality, Help mechanism, LL/SC instruction, Memory location, Non-blocking, Obstruction-freedom, Progress condition, Sequential specification, k-Set agreement, k-Simultaneous consensus, Speculative execution, Universal construction, Wait-freedom.

1.1   INTRODUCTION

1.1.1   A VERY SHORT HISTORICAL PERSPECTIVE

At the very beginning   Looking for (some) universality seems inherent to humankind. Any language, any writing system, can be seen as an attempt toward universality [88, 105]. In the science domain, one of the very first witnesses of research of universality found in the past seems to be the Plimpton 322 tablet (Figure 1.1), which describes the first 15 Pythagorean triplets $(a^2 + b^2 = c^2)$. This is only a list, not yet an algorithm with its proof. Hence, this tablet is a step to universality for Pythagorean triplets, but not yet a universal method able to provide us with a sequence of Pythagorean triplets of any length.

Geometric constructions   The geometric constructions with a compass and a straightedge designed by the Ancient Greeks are among the first algorithms coming with a correctness proof (see also [105]). The operations defining this computing model[1] are:

- with the straightedge: draw a line,

- with the compass:

---
[1]The notion of a *computing* model is discussed in [94, 129].

Figure 1.1: Plimpton 322 tablet.

- draw a circle or an arc of a circle,

- copy the length of a segment.

To illustrate geometric constructions, let us consider the very simple problem which consists in bisecting an angle (i.e., dividing an angle into two equal sub-angles). Such a construction (algorithm), described in Figure 1.2 where the vertex of the angle is denoted A, consists of the following steps.

- Draw an arc of a circle of center A (top left of the figure). This arc cuts the sides of the angles in B and C. The radius of the circle can be arbitrary, say r_1.

- Draw a circle of center B, and a circle of center C, with the same radius r_2 such that the two circles intersect at a point D and draw the segments BD and BC (bottom right of the figure).

- Finally, draw a line from A to a point where the two circles of radius r_2 intersect (bottom left of the figure). So we have two triangles ABD and ACD.

- Claim: the angles $\widehat{BAD}$ and $\widehat{DAC}$ are equal.

The proof of the claim is easy. As $|AB| = |AC| = r_1$, $|BD| = |CD| = r_2$, and the side AD is common to the two triangles, it follows that the triangles BAD and DAC are equal. So, the corresponding angles are equal from which follows $\widehat{BAD} = \widehat{DAC}$.

Is every geometric construction possible?   Proving that some geometric constructions are impossible in the "compass + straightedge" computing model took a long time. The most famous

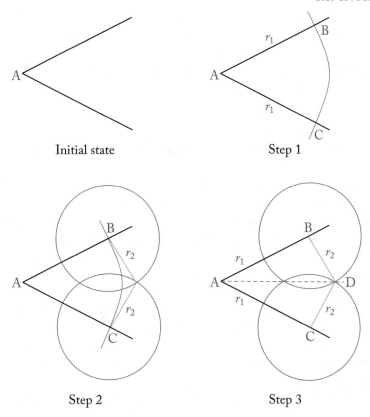

Figure 1.2: An algorithm to bisect an angle.

example is the impossibility of squaring the circle, i.e., build, with straightedge and compass only, a square whose area is equal to the area of a given circle.[2]

From Euclid to Turing Considering base operations that can be mechanically realized (e.g., [87, 102, 132]), a Turing machine provides us with an abstract computing device, which is considered as the most general sequential computing model, thereby fixing limits of what can be computed by a sequential machine [139].[3] It is consequently claimed to be *universal*. The *halting* problem is the most famous of the problems that are impossible to solve in this "most general" sequential computing model.

---

[2]This impossibility follows from the fact that π is a transcendent number (F. von Lindemann 1882), and a theorem by P. L. Wantzel, who established, in 1837, necessary and sufficient conditions for a number to be constructed in the "compass + straightedge" computing model [140].

[3]This means that any sequential computing model proposed so far has the same computability power as a Turing machine (e.g., Church's Lambda calculus, or Post systems [110]), or is weaker than a Turing machine (e.g., finite state automata).

On the nature of Informatics   A scientific domain should not be confused with its many applications. Algorithmics (i.e., the study of algorithms, what they can do, which are their limits, etc.) lies at the center of Informatics. An algorithm is intimately related to the computing model for which it has been designed. As far as sequential computing is concerned, the reader will find in [65] a very nice introduction to the *spirit of algorithms*.

1.1.2   ON THE NATURE OF DISTRIBUTED COMPUTING

The aim of *parallel computing* is to exploit data independence to produce efficient computations.[4] The nature of distributed computing is totally different. Born around the early 1980s, its aim is to allow pre-defined independent computing entities to cooperate in the realization of a common goal. It is important to notice that the computing entities (processes) are not under the control of the programmers, they are imposed to them. The main difficulty of distributed computing comes from the *environment* in which the computing entities evolve. The behavior of the environment (asynchrony, mutiplicity of control flows, occurrence of failures, mobility, etc.) is not under the control of the computing entities and can be seen as a set of adversaries that strive to prevent the computing entities to cooperate.

It appears that, when considering a distributed algorithm A executed in a given environment E (also called *context*[5]), the actual behavior of the environment E during each execution execution of A constitutes an implicit (or hidden) input of that execution of A. Mastering one form or another of the *uncertainty* created by the environment constitutes a major difficulty of distributed computing [120, 122].

It follows that some notions (such as computability) have a different flavor in sequential/parallel computing and distributed computing. More precisely, as written in [72]:

> "*In sequential systems, computability is understood through the Church–Turing Thesis: anything that can be computed, can be computed by a Turing Machine. In distributed systems, where computations require coordination among multiple participants, computability questions have a different flavor. Here, too, there are many problems which are not computable, but these limits to computability reflect the difficulty of making decisions in the face of ambiguity, and have little to do with the inherent computational power of individual participants.*"

In distributed computing the main issues posed by universality and computability appear when one has to implement distributed state machines (distributed services encapsulated in concurrent objects) in the presence of adversaries due to the environment in which the computation evolves (such as asynchrony and process failures) [50, 66, 91, 96].

---

[4]Let us observe that, if one is not interested in efficiency, any problem that can solved by a parallel algorithm can be solved by a sequential algorithm. This is no longer true in distributed computing. As an example, the *distributed termination detection* has no meaning in sequential computing [117].

[5]Which constitues a part of the *computing model*.

1.1.3   BASIC ASYNCHRONOUS READ/WRITE MODEL $\mathcal{CARW}_{n,t}[\emptyset]$

Definition   The basic computing model $\mathcal{CARW}_{n,t}[\emptyset]$ is composed of a set of n sequential and asynchronous processes $p_1, \ldots, p_n$ in which at most $t < n$ processes may crash (see below). "Sequential" means that a process executes operations one after the other as specified by its algorithm. "Asynchronous" means that each process proceeds at its own speed, which can be arbitrary and remains always unknown to the other processes.

A process *crash* is a premature and definitive halt. Hence, a process executes correctly its local algorithm until it possibly crashes. Due to the atomicity of the hardware-provided operations (here read and write operations), if a process crashes while executing such an operation, this operation appears as entirely executed or not at all. A process that crashes in a run is said to be *faulty* in this run. Otherwise, it is *correct* or *non-faulty*. Hence, a faulty process is a process whose speed, after some time, remains forever equal to 0.

Notation   The acronym $\mathcal{CARW}_n$ stands for "Crash Asynchronous Read/Write." The notation $[\emptyset]$ means that the only way for the processes to communicate is by reading and writing shared registers (memory locations of bounded size). This model is known under the name *wait-free read/write* model. As (by construction) $t < n$, the notations $\mathcal{CARW}_{n,t}[\emptyset]$ and $\mathcal{CARW}_{n,t}[t < n]$ are equivalent. The notation $\mathcal{CARW}_{n,t}[\text{Assumptions}]$ will be used later to add specific computability assumptions or restrictions on t to the basic model.

1.1.4   ON ATOMICITY

As just indicated, the processes communicate by accessing atomic read/write registers (memory locations). Atomicity means that the read and write primitive operations on a register appear as if they have been executed one after the other (in agreement with what would be seen by an omniscient external observer). Moreover, the corresponding sequence of operations S is such that [92]:

- real-time compliance: if a read or write operation op_1 terminated before another operation op_2 started, op_1 appears before op_2 in S; and

- semantics of the register: a read operation on a register R returns the value written by the closest preceding write operation on R (or its initial value if there is no preceding write) [92].

Atomicity is also called *linearizability* when considering any object defined by a sequential specification [76].

An execution of a multi-writer multi-reader (MWMR) atomic register accessed by three processes p_1, p_2, and p_3 is depicted in Figure 1.3 using a classical space-time diagram. $R.\text{read}() \rightarrow v$ means that the corresponding read operation returns the value v. Consequently, an external observer sees the following sequential execution of the register R which satisfies the

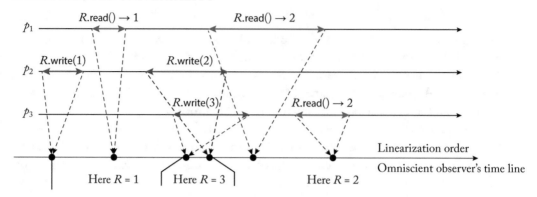

Figure 1.3: An execution of an atomic read/write register R.

definition of an atomic register:

$$R.\mathsf{write}(1),\ R.\mathsf{read}() \rightarrow 1,\ R.\mathsf{write}(3),\ R.\mathsf{write}(2),\ R.\mathsf{read}() \rightarrow 2,\ R.\mathsf{read}() \rightarrow 2.$$

Let us observe that $R.\mathsf{write}(3)$ and $R.\mathsf{write}(2)$ are concurrent, which means that they could appear to an external observer as if $R.\mathsf{write}(2)$ was executed before $R.\mathsf{write}(3)$. If this was the case, the execution would be correct if the last two read invocations (issued by p_1 and p_3) return the value 3, i.e., the external observer should then see the following sequential execution:

$$R.\mathsf{write}(1),\ R.\mathsf{read}() \rightarrow 1,\ R.\mathsf{write}(2),\ R.\mathsf{write}(3),\ R.\mathsf{read}() \rightarrow 3,\ R.\mathsf{read}() \rightarrow 3.$$

Let us also observe that the second read invocation by p_1 is concurrent with both $R.\mathsf{write}(2)$ and $R.\mathsf{write}(3)$. This means that it could appear as having been executed before these two write operations or even between them.

If it appears as having been executed before these two write operations, it should return the value 1 in order for the register behavior be atomic. As shown by these possible scenarios, *concurrency* is intimately related to *non-determinism*. It is not possible to predict which execution will be produced; it is only possible to enumerate the set of possible executions that could be produced (we can only predict that the one that is actually produced is one of them).

Why atomicity is fundamental: composability for free   Atomicity is a fundamental concept because it allows the composition of shared objects for free (i.e., their composition is at no additional cost). This means that, when considering two (or more) atomic registers $R1$ and $R2$, the composite object $[R1, R2]$ which is made up of $R1$ and $R2$ and provides the processes with the four operations $R1.\mathsf{read}()$, $R1.\mathsf{write}()$, $R2.\mathsf{read}()$, and $R2.\mathsf{write}()$ is also atomic. Everything appears as if at most one operation at a time was executed (on $R1$ or $R2$), and the sub-sequence including only the operations on $R1$ is a correct behavior of $R1$, and similarly for $R2$.

Notation   Variables local to a process p_i are denoted with lowercase letters, sometimes indexed with i. Memory location and objects shared by the processes are denoted with capital letters.

1.1.5   CONCURRENT OBJECTS

A concurrent object is an object that can be accessed (possibly simultaneously) by several processes. From both practical and theoretical point of views, a fundamental problem of concurrent programming consists in implementing high level concurrent objects, where "high level" means that the object provides the processes with an abstraction level higher than the atomic hardware-provided instructions. While this is well-known and well-mastered since a long time in the context of failure-free systems [27], it is far from being trivial in failure-prone systems (e.g., see textbooks such as [74, 116, 133]).

1.1.6   ON PROGRESS CONDITIONS

Deadlock-freedom and starvation-freedom are the well-known progress conditions traditionally considered in the context of failure-free asynchronous systems. As their implementation is based on lock mechanisms, they are not suited to asynchronous crash-prone systems. This is due to the fact that it is impossible to distinguish a crashed process from a slow process and, consequently, a process that acquires a lock and crashes before releasing it can entail the blocking of the entire system.

Hence, new progress conditions for concurrent objects suited to crash-prone asynchronous systems have been proposed. Given an object, we have the following.

- The strongest progress condition is *wait-freedom* (WF) [66]. It states that any operation (on the object that is built) invoked by a correct process always terminates.[6] This progress condition can be seen as the equivalent of the starvation-freedom progress condition encountered in failure-free systems.

- The *non-blocking* progress condition (NB) states that there is at least one process that can always progress (all its object operations terminate) [76]. This progress condition is also called *lock-freedom*. It can be seen as the equivalent of deadlock-freedom in failure-free systems. Non-blocking has been generalized in [28], under the name *k-lock-freedom* (k-NB), which states that at least k processes can always make progress.

- The *obstruction-freedom* progress condition (OB) states that a process that does not crash will be able to terminate its operation if all the other processes hold still long enough [69]. This is the weakest progress condition. It has been generalized in [134], under the name *k-obstruction-freedom* (k-OB), which states that, if a set of at most

---

[6]The fact that an operation issued by a correct process must always terminate (no matter how the other processes behave, whether they are correct or faulty) was first introduced in Lamport's seminal work on "concurrent reading and writing" [90], and later investigated in [109].

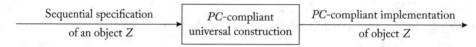

Figure 1.4: *PC*-compliant universal construction.

k processes run alone for a sufficiently long period of time, they will terminate their operations.

While *wait-freedom* and *non-blocking* are independent of the concurrency and failure pattern, *obstruction-freedom* is dependent from it. Asymmetric progress conditions have been introduced in [84]. The computational structure of progress conditions is investigated in [138]. The notion of *x*-wait-freedom ($1 \leq x < n$) has been introduced in [81]. This notion takes into account the notion of *vulnerability window* (the crash of a process can prevent the global progress of a distributed algorithm *A* only when that process executes some (as small as possible) predefined parts of *A*).

1.1.7   UNIVERSAL CONSTRUCTION

The notion of a universal construction was introduced by M. Herlihy in [66]. It considers objects (a) which are defined from sequential specifications and (b) whose operations are total, i.e., any object operation returns a result (as an example, a push() operation on an empty stack returns the default value $\perp$).

Let *PC* be a progress condition (WF, NB, OB). A *PC-compliant universal construction* is an algorithm that, given the sequential specification of an object *O* (or a sequential implementation of it), provides a concurrent implementation of *O* satisfying the progress condition *PC* in the presence of up $(n-1)$ process crashes (Figure 1.4).

It has been shown in [50, 66, 97] that the design of a universal construction with respect to the wait-freedom progress condition is impossible in $\mathcal{CARW}_{n,t}[\emptyset]$. This means that the basic system model $\mathcal{CARW}_{n,t}[\emptyset]$ has to be enriched with hardware-provided atomic instructions or additional computing objects whose computational power is stronger than atomic read/write registers (in the following, we consider terms "register" and "memory location" as synonyms; we sometimes also say "atomic read/write object" by a slight abuse of language).

This chapter is a guided tour to distributed universal constructions. Its goal is not to present as many universal constructions as possible, but to focus on the central features universal constructions rest on, and illustrate them with universal construction algorithms.

1.2   AN LL/SC-BASED WAIT-FREE UNIVERSAL CONSTRUCTION

This section presents a simple universal construction suited to the system model $CARW_{n,t}[\text{LL/SC}]$ (which is $CARW_{n,t}[\emptyset]$ enriched with the hardware-provided instructions LL and SC defined below). This allows for an easy introduction to the notion of a *speculative computation* and the notion of a *help mechanism* (introduced in [66] and recently formalized in [33]). This section also presents extensions devoted to *large* objects.

1.2.1   EXTENDING $CARW_{n,t}[\emptyset]$ WITH LL/SC

Model $CARW_{n,t}[\text{LL/SC}]$ These hardware-provided atomic instructions can be applied to any memory location. As already indicated, the wait-free read/write model $CARW_{n,t}[\emptyset]$ enriched with them is denoted $CARW_{n,t}[\text{LL/SC}]$. LL/SC is made up of two atomic operations where LL stands for Linked Load and SC stands for Store Conditional. Let X be a memory location.

- $X.\text{LL}()$ returns the current value of X.

- Let p_i be a process that invokes $X.\text{SC}(v)$. This invocation assigns v to X if X has not been assigned a value by another process since the previous invocation of $X.\text{LL}()$ issued by p_i. In this case, $X.\text{SC}(v)$ returns true and we say that the invocation is successful, otherwise it returns false.

Let us notice that, given a location (shared register) X, the invocation operation $X.\text{SC}()$ by a process p_i assumes that p_i has previously invoked $X.\text{LL}()$. Moreover between $X.\text{LL}()$ and the associated $X.\text{SC}()$ the process p_i can invoke $Y.\text{LL}()$ and $Y.\text{SC}()$ on any number of registers $Y \neq X$.

Notion of a speculative execution   These instructions are used to bracket a *speculative computation*. A process first reads X with $X.\text{LL}()$ and stores its value in a local variable x_i. Then p_i does a local computation which depends on both x_i and its local state. The aim of this local computation is to define a new value v for X. Finally, p_i tries to commit its local computation by writing v into X, which is done by invoking $X.\text{SC}(v)$. If this invocation is successful, the write is committed; otherwise the write fails. A similar behavior can be obtained by the Compare&swap() instruction.

The main advantage of LL/SC, with respect to Compare&swap(), lies in the fact that LL/SC does suffer the ABA problem (see [116, 133]), which requires sequence numbers to be solved. Algorithms based on LL/SC can be found in many publications (e.g., [48, 67, 79, 116, 133, 134] to cite a few).

1.2.2   A SIMPLE WAIT-FREE UNIVERSAL CONSTRUCTION IN $\mathcal{CARW}_{n,t}[\text{LL/SC}]$

This section presents a simplified version (denoted as sFK) of a universal construction due to P. Fatourou and N. Kallimanis [49]. The main difference is that the presented construction uses sequence numbers which increase forever, while [49] uses sequence numbers modulo 2. This additional memory cost makes it much easier to present, understand, and prove correct.

Specification of the object O that is built   The object O is assumed to be defined by a transition function $\delta()$. Let s be the current state of O and $\text{op}(in_i)$ be the invocation of the operation $\text{op}()$ on O, with input parameter in; $\delta(s, \text{op}(in))$ outputs a pair $\langle s', r \rangle$ such that s' is the state of O after the execution of $\text{op}(in)$ on s, and r is the result of $\text{op}(in)$. To simplify, it is assumed that the object is deterministic, i.e., given an invocation $\text{op}(in_i))$, $\delta(s, \text{op}(in))$ has a single output.

Local variables at process p_i   Each process p_i manages:

- a local integer sn_i (initialized to 1) to generate sequence numbers and

- the following auxiliary variables: ls_i, r_i, new_state_i plus a local array $pairs_i$.

Shared registers implementing the object O

- $STATE$ is a memory location made up of three fields:

    - $STATE.value$ contains the current value of O. It is initialized to the initial value of O.

    - $STATE.sn[1..n]$ is an array of sequence numbers initialized to $[0, \ldots, 0]$; $STATE.sn[i]$ is the sequence number of the last invocation of an operation on O issued by p_i.

    - $STATE.res[1..n]$ is an array of result values initialized to $[\bot, \ldots, \bot]$; $STATE.res[i]$ contains the result of the last operation issued by p_i that has been applied to O.

- $BOARD[1..n]$ is an array of atomic single-writer multi-reader registers. $BOARD[i]$ can be read by all the processes but written only by p_i. It is made up of a pair $\langle BOARD[i].op, BOARD[i].sn \rangle$ initialized to $\langle \bot, 0 \rangle$. $BOARD[i].op$ contains the last operation on the object O issued by p_i, and $BOARD[i].sn$ contains the associated sequence number.

LL/SC-based universal construction: speculative computation and helping   The construction is described in Algorithm 1.1. When a process p_i invokes an operation $\text{op}(in_i)$ on O, it first publishes the pair $\langle \text{op}(in_i), sn_i \rangle$ in the collect object $BOARD$ (line 1). Then, it invokes the internal procedure $\text{apply}()$ at the end of which it will locally return the result produced by $\text{op}(in_i)$ (line 5).

Algorithm 1.1 Wait-free universal construction in the system model $\mathcal{CARW}_{n,t}$[LL/SC]

---

when p_i **invokes** op(in_i) **do**
(1) $BOARD[i] \leftarrow \langle op(in_i), sn_i \rangle$;
(2) $sn_i \leftarrow sn_i + 1$;
(3)   apply();
(4) $r_i \leftarrow STATE.res[i]$;
(5)   return(r_i)
end of invocation.

internal operation apply() **is**
(6)   **repeat twice**
(7) $ls_i \leftarrow STATE.LL()$;
(8) $pairs_i \leftarrow [BOARD[1], ..., BOARD[n]]$;   % asynchronous collect() operation
(9)   **for** $\ell \in \{1, 2, ..., n\}$ **do**
(10)   **if** $(pairs_i[\ell].sn = ls_i.sn[\ell] + 1)$ **then**
(11) $\langle new\_state_i, r_i \rangle \leftarrow \delta(ls_i.value, pairs_i[\ell].op)$;
(12) $ls_i.res[\ell] \leftarrow r; ls_i.sn[\ell] \leftarrow pairs_i[\ell].sn$
(13)   **end if**
(14)   **end for;**
(15) $STATE.SC(ls_i)$
(16)   **end repeat twice**
end of internal operation.

The core of the construction is the procedure apply(), in which a process p_i executes lines 4–12 twice (we will see later why this has to be done twice). Process p_i first reads the current local state of the object (line 7), and starts a first speculative execution (which will end at line 15). In this speculative execution, p_i first reads the content of the collect object $BOARD$ from which it obtains for each process p_ℓ a pair $\langle$last operation invoked by p_ℓ, associated sequence number$\rangle$. Let us recall that, while the read of each entry of $BOARD$ is atomic, the read of the whole array done at line 8 is not atomic. Hence, the pairs that are returned to p_i are not necessarily associated with a consistent global state the computation passed through.

Then, p_i considers each pair in $pairs_i$ in the "for" loop of lines 9–14. In this loop, p_i strives to help all the processes that have a pending operation on O. From its point of view (i.e., with the information it has obtained from its previous reads of $STATE$ and $BOARD$), those are all the processes p_ℓ such that $pairs_i[\ell].sn = ls.sn[\ell] + 1$ (line 10). If this local predicate is true, p_i locally simulates (speculative computation) the last operation issued by p_ℓ not yet applied to the object (line 11), and locally saves the result of the operation and its sequence number (line 12). Finally, p_i tries to commit its speculative computation by invoking $STATE.SC()$ (line 15). Let us observe that, if this invocation is successful, we can conclude that no process modified $STATE$ while p_i was doing its speculative computation. Hence, the local variable ls_i of p_i is up to date, and, from an external observer point of view, everything appears as if the computation starting at line 7 and ending at line 15 was executed atomically. If the invocation of $STATE.SC()$ is not successful, the speculative execution is not committed.

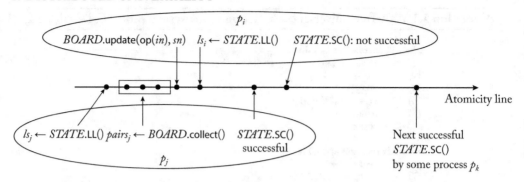

Figure 1.5: Why to repeat lines 7–15 twice (big dot = atomic step).

Construction based on LL/SC: why "repeat twice"? Let us first observe that, due to sequence numbers, once registered in the collect object *BOARD*, an operation cannot be executed more than once. Moreover, if the process p_i that invokes an operation does not crash, it terminates its operation op(in). This follows from the fact that lines 10–13 are executed a bounded number of times ($2n$). But is the result provided for op(in) correct?

To answer this question, let us consider the execution described in Figure 1.5. When process p_j (bottom of the figure) executes the atomic statement *STATE*.LL() followed by the asynchronous read of *BOARD*[i] (lines 7–8), p_i (top of the figure) has not yet registered by writing ⟨op(in), sn⟩ in *BOARD*[i] (line 1). Hence, $pairs_j$ does not contain ⟨op(in), sn⟩. Let us assume that the execution of *STATE*.SC(ls_j) by p_j is successful. If p_i executes only once the repeat loop, its execution of *STATE*.SC() is not successful, and p_i returns despite the fact that p_j has not helped it by executing op(in). Hence, the statement return(r_i) executed by p_i at line 5 returns the result of its previous operation invocation.

Assuming now that p_i executes the repeat loop twice, let us consider the first successful invocation of *STATE*.SC() that occurs after the previous successful invocation by p_j. This invocation is issued by some process p_k (which can be p_i, p_j or any other process). According to the algorithm of Figure 1.1, it follows that p_k has previously invoked *STATE*.LL(). Moreover, this invocation occurs necessarily after the successful invocation of *STATE*.SC() by p_j (otherwise the invocation of *STATE*.SC() by p_k could not be successful). Consequently, the invocation of *BOARD*.collect() by p_k (at line 8) is such that ⟨op(in), sn⟩ ∈ $pairs_k$. It follows that p_k found $pairs_k[i].sn = ls_k.sn[i] + 1$, and simulated the execution of op(in) on behalf of p_i and wrote the corresponding result in $ls_k.res[i]$ which was then copied in *STATE*.res[i] by the successful execution of *STATE*.SC() by p_k.

Linearization of the operations on O Let SC[1], SC[2], ..., SC[x], etc. be the sequence of all the successful invocations of *STATE*.SC(). As *STATE*.SC() is atomic, this sequence is well-defined. Starting from $SC[1]$, each SC[x] applies at least one operation on the object O. It is possible to totally order the operations applied to O by each SC[x]. Let seq[x] be the corresponding sequence. The sequence of operations applied to O is then seq[1] followed by seq[2], ..., followed by seq[x], etc.

Remark on sequence numbers Techniques such as the one described in [17, 98] (known under the name *alternating bit protocol*) can be used to obtain an implementation in which the sequence numbers are implemented modulo 2.

1.2.3   FROM WEAK-LL/SC TO LL/SC

Weak-LL/SC Some machines present weak versions of the pair of LL/SC operations. These versions use cache invalidation mechanisms which do not distinguish operations on different registers, which can cause SC() invocations to spuriously return `false`. So an important issue consists in building the pair of operations LL/SC on top of the such weak WLL/WSC operations while they should return `true`. In the following, we consider the pair of WLL/WSC operations defined as follows: They behave as LL/SC except for the following points where X is a shared register [101].

- Access pattern limitation. Between a pair of consecutive operations X.WLL() and X.WSC() issued by a process p_i, this process does not access the shared memory (so between X.WLL() and X.WSC() it can access only local variables).

- Finitely many spurious failures. A finite number of invocations X.WSC() may fail (so they return `false`) while the corresponding invocation of X.SC() would have returned `true` (so these spurious failures are transient failures).

The differences between WLL/*wsc* and LL/SC are illustrated in Figure 1.6. WLL/WSC captures the main difference between what is provided by the hardware and what we want to have, namely LL/SC. In the top line (LL/SC operations) there are no constraints on operation invocations, while there are on the bottom line (WLL/WSC operations).

Algorithm 1.2 builds the pair LL/SC on top of the base operations WLL/WSC. The shared register X is composed of two fields: a value X.*value* initialized to the initial value of X if any, and a sequence number X.*sn* initialized to 0. The invocation of X.LL() is a simple call of X.WLL() which returns the current value of X and saves it in the local variable x_i.

The invocation of X.SC(*new*) first builds the pair $\langle x_i.sn + 1, new \rangle$ (line 3), where $x_i.sn + 1$ would be the sequence number associated with the value *new* if the conditional write succeeds. Then p_i enters a loop (lines 4–8). If it finds that X has been modified since its last invocation of X.LL(), p_i returns the value `false` (line 5). If X has not been modified p_i invokes (X.WSC(y_i)) to try to write the next pair in X (line 6). If it succeeds it returns `true`. If it fails, it re-enters the loop.

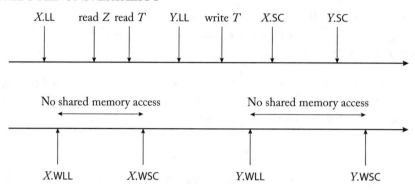

Figure 1.6: WLL/WSC vs. LL/SC.

Algorithm 1.2 Wait-free LL/SC register in the system model $\mathcal{CARW}_{n,t}$[WLL/WSC]

$$
\begin{aligned}
&\textbf{operation } X.\text{LL}() \textbf{ is} \qquad\qquad\qquad \%\ \text{code for process } p_i \\
&(1)\qquad x_i \leftarrow X.\text{WLL}(); \\
&(2)\qquad \text{return}(x_i.value) \\
&\textbf{end of operation.}
\end{aligned}
$$

$$
\begin{aligned}
&\textbf{operation } X.\text{SC}(new) \textbf{ is} \\
&(3)\qquad y_i \leftarrow \langle (x_i.sn) + 1, new \rangle; \\
&(4)\qquad \textbf{while } (\text{true}) \textbf{ do} \\
&(5)\qquad\quad \textbf{if } (X.\text{WLL}() \neq x_i) \textbf{ then } \text{return}(\text{false}) \\
&(6)\qquad\qquad \textbf{else if } (X.\text{WSC}(y_i)) \textbf{ then } \text{return}(\text{true}) \textbf{ end if} \\
&(7)\qquad\quad \textbf{end if} \\
&(8)\qquad \textbf{end while} \\
&\textbf{end of operation.}
\end{aligned}
$$

1.3   AN MMSWAP-BASED WAIT-FREE UNIVERSAL CONSTRUCTION

1.3.1   EXTENDING $\mathcal{CARW}$[Ø] WITH MMSWAP

The operation MMswap() is an operation that atomically exchanges the content of two registers. Let X and Y be two shared registers, whose values are a and b, respectively. After the invocation of MMswap(X, Y) we have $X = b$ and $Y = a$.

In the following, $\mathcal{CARW}$[MMswap] denotes the basic model $\mathcal{CARW}$[Ø] enriched with MMswap().

1.3.2   A WAIT-FREE UNIVERSAL CONSTRUCTION IN $\mathcal{CARW}$[MMswap]

This section presents a wait-free universal construction for the model $\mathcal{CARW}$[MMswap] due to M. Perrin and A. Mostéfaoui [18].

Notations   The following algorithm uses a list of records, each record of the list including a pointer to the previous record. Let X be an record of the list. $\uparrow X$ denotes a pointer to X. If Y contains a pointer, $Y \downarrow$ denotes the record pointed to by Y. (Hence, $\uparrow (Y \downarrow) = Y$ and $(\uparrow X) \downarrow = X$.)

The object O that is built and its internal representation   As in Section 1.2.2, the object O to build is assumed to be deterministic and specified by a transition function $\delta()$. Its internal representation is composed of:

- A list whose records are made up of four fields. Let *elt* be a record. We have:

    - *elt.op* contains the invocation of an operation on the object O with its parameters,

    - *elt.state* contains the value of O resulting from the execution of *elt.op*,

    - *elt.result* contains the result of the invocation of *elt.op*, and

    - *elt.previous* contains a pointer to the previous record of the list (or $\perp$ if there is no previous record).

- A pointer *LAST* which points to the last record of the list.

The list is initially made up of a single record $\langle \perp, s_0, \perp, \perp \rangle$ (where s_0 is the initial value of O) and *LAST* points to this record.

Algorithm 1.3 Wait-free universal construction in the system model $\mathcal{CARW}_{n,t}[\text{MMswap}]$

---

when p_i invokes op(in_i) do
(1)   Allocation of a new shared register X_i;
(2) $X_i \leftarrow \langle \text{op}(in_i), \perp, \perp, \uparrow X_i \rangle$;
(3)   MMswap($LAST, X_i.previous$);
(4)   apply(X_i);
(5) $res_i \leftarrow X_i.result$;
(6)   return(res_i)
end of operation.

internal operation apply(X) **is**
(7) $y_i \leftarrow X.previous$;
(8)   **if** ($y_i \neq \perp$) **then**
(9)   apply($y_i \downarrow$);
(10) $(X.state, X.result) \leftarrow \delta((X.previous \downarrow).state, X.operation)$;
(11) $X.previous \leftarrow \perp$
(12)   **end if**
end of operation.

The MMswap-based universal construction   This construction is defined by Algorithm 1.3. When a process p_i invokes an operation op(in) on the object O, it first obtains a shared register X_i (line 1) in which it deposits a record that will be become a record of the list implementing the object O. This record is $\langle \text{op}(in), \perp, \perp, \uparrow X_i \rangle$. Let us notice that the last field is a pointer to the record itself (line 2). Then p_i invokes MMswap($LAST$, $X_i.previous$) (line 3) which atomically exchanges the pointers in $LAST$ and $X_i.previous$ (which is a pointer to X_i itself). Let us notice that, as MMswap() is atomic, if several processes concurrently invoke this operation, every occurs as if they have been executed in some sequential order. Then, p_i invokes the internal operation apply(X_i) described below. When apply(X_i) has terminated, p_i returns the result associated with its invocation of op(in) (line 6). The linearization order of the operations on the object O is defined by the order in which are linearized the atomic operation MMswap($LAST$, $-$).

When it executes the internal operation apply(X), a process p_i first extracts the pointer y_i contained in the record X (line 7). If this pointer is $\perp$, the corresponding operation has already been applied and apply(X) terminates. If $y_i \neq \perp$ (line 8), p_i considers the record pointed to by y_i and invokes apply() on it (line 9). This can recursively entail the execution of previous operations on O registered in the list but not yet executed. Let us notice that these operations on O are executed according to the total order defined by the list whose head is pointed to by $LAST$ (accessed by the atomic operation MMswap($LAST$, $-$). Then, when apply() terminates, p_i computes the new state of the object O ($X.state$) and the result ($X.result$) associated with the operation registered in the record X line 10). Finally, p_i sets $X.previous$ to $\perp$ (line 11), which indicates that all the operations registered in the previous records have been executed.

An example   Let us consider the processes p_1, p_2, and p_3 that invokes $O.op_1(in_1)$, $O.op_2(in_2)$, and $O.op_3(in_3)$, respectively. To simplify the writing $op_x(in_x)$ is shortened in op_x.

- At the initialization time, we have $LAST = G$ where G is a pointer to the record $\langle \perp, s_o, \perp, \perp \rangle$.

- At time $\tau_1 > \tau_0$, p_1 invokes op_1. So p_1 first deposits $\langle op_1, \perp, \perp, \uparrow X_1 \rangle$ in X_1 and invokes MMswap($LAST$, X_1). We have then $LAST = \uparrow X_1$ and $X_1 = \langle op_1, \perp, \perp, G \rangle$.

  Then, p_1 invokes apply(X_1). We have then $y_1 = X_1.previous$. Consequently, as $y_1 = G \neq \perp$, p_1 invokes apply(G) (line 9). As $G.previous = \perp$, this recursive invocation returns and p_1 executes lines 10–11, at the end which we have $X_1 = \langle op_1, s_1, r_1, \perp \rangle$ such that $s_1 = \delta(s_0, op_1)$ and r_1 is the result produced by op_1, that is returned by p_1 at line 6.

- At a later time, p_2 invokes op_2 which produces the record $X_2 = \langle op_2, \perp, \perp, \uparrow X_2 \rangle$, and p_3 invokes op_3 which produces the record $X_3 \langle op_3, \perp, \perp, \uparrow X_3 \rangle$.

- At a later time, p_2 and p_3 invoke simultaneously MMswap($LAST$, X_2) and MMswap($LAST$, X_3). Due to way the atomicity of MMswap(), two scenarios are possible: MMswap($LAST$, X_2) appears as being executed before MMswap($LAST$, X_3) orMMswap($LAST$, X_3) appears as being executed before MMswap($LAST$, X_2) (this non-determinism is due to concurrency). We consider here that MMswap($LAST$, X_2) appears as being ordered before MMswap($LAST$, X_3).

It follows that, after the execution MMswap($LAST, X_2$) we have $LAST =\uparrow X_2$ and $X_2 = \langle op_2, \perp, \perp, \uparrow X_1 \rangle$, and after the execution MMswap($LAST, X_3$) we have $LAST =\uparrow X_3$ and $X_3 = \langle op_3, \perp, \perp, \uparrow X_2 \rangle$.

- Let us now consider the scenario where p_2 pauses for some period of time. So, from now, only p_3 is running. It invokes apply(X_3). As $X_3 = \langle op_2, \perp, \perp, \uparrow X_2 \rangle$, we have $y_3 =\uparrow X2$. It follows that p_3 invokes apply(X_2). At the end of this recursive call we have $X_2 = \langle op_2, s_2, r_2, \perp \rangle$ and p_3 terminates its invocation of apply(X_3), at end of which we have $X_3 = \langle op_3, s_3, r_3, \perp \rangle$. Finally, p_3 returns r_3.

- Let us now assume that p_2 wakes up. It invokes apply(X_2) where $X_2 = \langle op_2, s_2, r_2, \perp \rangle$. As $X_2.previous = \perp$, p_3 terminates apply(X_3) without modifying any register, and when it executes line 6, it returns r_2 as the result of op_2.

- Let us observe that, as soon as an operation is registered in the list, it is eventually executed. This execution will be done either by the invoking process or by a another process that invokes an operation on the object 0.

1.3.3   COMPARING LL/SC AND MMSWAP

In order to implement an object O, the universal construction based on the pair LL/SC described in Figure 1.1 uses three arrays (denoted *STATE.sn*, *STATE.res*, and *BOARD*) whose size is n. Consequently, the shared memory cost of this construction is $O(n)$. This cost is *permanent* in the sense it is independent of the fact that processes invoke or not operations on the object O.

The situation is different in the universal construction based on the atomic operation MMswap described in Figure 1.3. When processes are invoking operations, the internal representation of the object O is a list whose size depends on the number of processes currently invoking operations on the object 0, which is at most n. In a very interesting way, when no process accesses the object O, the size of the list is reduced to 1 (only the last operation with the last state on O is registered).

1.4   EXTENSIONS
1.4.1   THE CASE OF LARGE OBJECTS

The previous universal construction considered that the internal state of the object (*STATE*) can be copied all at once. A *large* object is an object whose internal state cannot be copied in one instruction.

Several articles have addressed this problem, e.g., [2, 8, 67]. They all propose to fragment a large object into blocks. Two main approaches have been proposed.

- One consists in using pointers linking the blocks representing the object [67]. Moreover, it requires that the programmer provides a sequential implementation of the object that performs as little copying as possible. The pointers are then accessed with LL operations which allow a process to obtain a logical copy of the object (which means that only the needed part of the object is copied in its local memory). A process executes then locally a speculative computation, as defined by the operation it wants to apply to the object. Finally, it uses SC operations on the appropriate pointers to try to commit the new value of the object.

- The other approach consists in representing the object as a long array fragmented into blocks [8]. This paper presents two object constructions based on this approach, which are universal with respect to non-blocking and wait-freedom, respectively. It also presents algorithms implementing atomic LL/LSC operations (where "L" stands for Large), which extend the LL/SC operations to arrays of memory locations. These operations are built in the system model $\mathcal{CARW}_{n,t}$[LL/SC].

1.4.2   ON THE IMPLEMENTATION SIDE: DISJOINT-ACCESS PARALLELISM

Disjoint-access parallelism   A universal construction is *disjoint-access parallel* if two processes that access distinct parts of an object O do not access common base objects or common memory location which constitute the internal representation of O. As an example, let us consider a queue. If the queue contains three or more items, a process executing enqueue(v) and a process executing dequeue() must be able to progress without interfering.

Hence, the aim of a disjoint-access parallel universal construction is to provide efficient implementations. Let us observe that all the universal constructions that built a total order on the operations (such as the one described in Section 1.2.2 and the ones presented in [2, 48, 67]) are not disjoint-access parallel.

What can be done?   Hence the question posed by F. Ellen, P. Fatourou, N. Kosmas, A. Milani, and C. Travers in [46]: Is it possible to design a disjoint-access parallel WF-compliant universal construction? This work presents two important results.

- The first is an impossibility result. It states that it is impossible to design a universal construction that is disjoint-access parallel and ensures that all the operation invocations of the processes that do not crash always terminate. Hence, when we consider any object defined by a sequential specification, disjoint-access parallelism and wait-freedom are mutually exclusive.

- The second result is a positive one, namely the previous impossibility (which considers *any* object defined by a sequential specification) does not apply to a special class of concurrent objects. Hence, the constructions for this object class are no longer "universal" in the strict sense. This object class contains all the objects O for which, in any sequential execution, each operation accesses a bounded number of base objects used to represent O. Examples of such objects are bounded trees, or stacks and queues whose internal representations are list-based.

In their paper, the authors describe a universal construction that ensures, for the previous objects, both the disjoint-access parallel property of the object implementation, and the wait-freedom progress condition for the processes that use it. This construction is presented in the system model $CARW_{n,t}[LL/SC]$.

1.4.3 ON THE OBJECT SIDE: ABORTABLE OBJECTS

Abortable objects have been investigated in several articles, e.g., [6, 29, 64, 116, 118]. They found their origin in the commit/abort output of transaction-based systems [60], and the notion of *fast path* initially introduced by L. Lamport to solve fast mutual exclusion [93].

Definition An abortable object is an object (defined by a sequential specification) such that:

- when executed in a contention-free context, an operation takes effect, i.e., modifies the state of the object and returns a result as defined by its sequential specification; and

- when executed in a contention context, an operation either takes effect and returns a result as defined by its sequential specification, or returns the default value $\bot$ (abort). If $\bot$ is returned, the operation has no effect on the state of the object.

Hence, an abortable object is such that any operation always returns (i.e., whatever the concurrency context). Its progress condition is consequently wait-freedom. Differently from an abortable object, an obstruction-free object does not guarantee operation termination in the presence of concurrency. A theory of deterministic abortable objects (including a study of their respective power) is presented in [64].

Universal constructions for abortable objects Algorithm 1.4 describes such a very simple construction. It is a trivial simplification of the universal construction described in Algorithm 1.1 from which the helping mechanism has been suppressed. The memory location *STATE* contains now only the state of the object.

Algorithm 1.4 Wait-free universal construction for abortable objects in the model $CARW_{n,t}[LL/SC]$

```
when p_i invokes op(in_i) do                        % code for p_i
(1)      ls_i ← STATE.LL();
(2)      ⟨new_state_i, r_i⟩ ← δ(ls_i, op(in_i));
(3)      done_i ← STATE.SC(new_state_i);
(4)      if (done_i) then return(r_i) else return(⊥) end if
end of invocation.
```

When a process p_i invokes an operation op(in) on the object, it reads its current state to obtain a local copy ls_i (line 1). Then it produces a speculative execution of op(in) on this local state ls_i (line 2). Finally, it tries to commit its local execution by issuing *STATE*.SC(ls_i) (line 3). If this SC is successful, the speculative execution is committed and consequently p_i returns the result r_i it has previously computed. Otherwise, there was at least one concurrent operation, and p_i returns $\bot$ (line 4).

Let us observe that, if several processes concurrently invoke operations, each invokes *STATE*.LL(), and the first of them that invokes *STATE*.SC() produces a successful SC. It follows that, in the presence of concurrency, at least one process is guaranteed to make progress in the sense that it does not return $\bot$.

An efficient *solo-fast* universal construction for deterministic abortable objects is described in [29]. Solo-fast (also called contention-aware in other articles) means that the implementation is allowed to use atomic operations on memory locations stronger than read/write only when there is contention. Moreover, this implementation guarantees that the operations that do not modify the object never return $\bot$ and use only read/write operations. This implementation is based on the primitive operation on memory locations Compare&swap, whose computational power is the same as LL/SC.

k-Abortable objects   This notion has been introduced in [20]. A k-*abortable* object guarantees progress even under high contention, where "progress" means that $\bot$ cannot be returned by some operation invocations.

Roughly speaking, an operation invoked by a process is allowed to abort only if it is concurrent with operations issued by k distinct processes and none of them returns $\bot$. This means that the k operations that entail the abort of another operation must succeed. It is easy to see that n-abortability is wait-freedom where any operation returns a non-$\bot$ result. A formal presentation can be found in [20].

A universal construction for k-abortable objects suited to the system model $\mathcal{CARW}_{n,t}$[LL/SC] is presented in [20]. Differently from the trivial construction for abortable objects presented in Figure 1.4, it is not a trivial construction. It uses an array of n memory locations $BOARD[1..n]$ used by the processes to store their last operations (they are the equivalent of the collect object $BOARD[1..n]$ used in Figure 1.1), an array of k memory locations $WINNERS[1..k]$ which contains the (up to k) "winning" operations, and another memory location $STATE$ (similar to the location $STATE$ used in Figure 1.1). All these memory locations are accessed with the LL/SC atomic operations. (We use the same identifiers as in Algorithm 1.1 to facilitate the understanding.)

The construction works as follows. After it has registered its operation in $BOARD[i]$, a process p_i tries to find an available entry in $WINNERS[1..k]$. If it succeeds, its operation will not abort; otherwise its operation will eventually abort. In all cases, i.e., whatever the fate of its own operation, the process p_i will help the winning operations to terminate. This construction is efficient in the sense that each operation terminates in $O(k)$ accesses to memory locations.

Let us observe that, as every k-abortable object can easily implement its k-lock-free counterpart, the previous universal construction for k-abortable objects is k-NB-compliant universal construction. Let us remember that, differently from its k-lock-free counterpart, no process can get stuck when a k-abortable object is used.

1.5   FROM OPERATIONS ON MEMORY LOCATIONS TO AGREEMENT OBJECTS

1.5.1   PRIMITIVE OPERATIONS vs. OBJECTS

The previous universal constructions are based on hardware-provided atomic operations such as LL/SC.

As all the hardware-provided synchronization operations (e.g., Test&Set or Compare&swap) the LL/SC operations are uniform in the sense that they can be applied to any memory location [8, 47]. Hence, the following natural questions come to mind:

- Is it possible to design a universal construction with other hardware-provided atomic operations such as Test&Set or Fetch&add, initially designed to solve synchronization issues? Moreover, which atomic operations are equivalent (i.e., which atomic operations have the same computational power from the point of view of a universal construction)?

- Is it possible to generalize the concept of a universal construction to the coordinated construction of several objects with different progress conditions?

The first question will be addressed in Chapter 2, while the answer to the second question is given below. The answer to both questions rely on the most famous object of fault-tolerant distributed computing, namely the *consensus* object.

1.5.2   A FUNDAMENTAL AGREEMENT OBJECT: CONSENSUS

Differently from a memory location which is only a sequence of bits accessed by hardware-provided atomic operations, the aim of an object is to provide its users with a high abstraction level (by hiding implementation details) and allow easier reasoning and proofs. An object is defined by a set of operations, and a specification (expressed as a set of properties on the operations of the object) which describes its correct behaviors. Due to its very definition the operations associated with an object are specific to it.

The consensus object   The consensus object is the fundamental object associated with agreement problems. Introduced (in a different form) in the context of Byzantine synchronous message-passing systems [96], a consensus object provides the processes with a single operation denoted propose() that a process can invoke only once (hence a consensus object is a one-shot object). When a process invokes propose(v), we say that it "proposes the value v." This operation returns a result. If a process returns value w, we say that the process "decides w." In the context of process crash failures, the consensus object is defined by the following set of properties (let us recall that a correct process is a process that does not crash).

- Termination. If a correct process invokes propose(), it decides a value.

- Validity. A decided value is a proposed value.

- Agreement. No two processes decide different values.

A consensus object allows the processes to agree on the same value, and this value is not arbitrary: it was proposed by one of them. Hence, when considering a universal construction, consensus objects can be used by the processes to agree on the order in which their operations must be applied to the object that is built.

1.5.3   IMPLEMENTING WAIT-FREE CONSENSUS IN ENRICHED $\mathcal{CARW}_{n,t}[\emptyset]$ MODELS

This section presents two constructions of a consensus object in a system of n processes for any value of n. Both are based on *conditional write* underlying operations.

Building wait-free consensus in $\mathcal{CARW}_{n,t}[\text{LL/SC}]$ The pair of atomic operations LL/SC has been defined in Section 1.2.1. Algorithm 1.5 builds a consensus object in the model $\mathcal{CARW}_{n,t}[\text{LL/SC}]$. The shared register VAL will contain the value decided by the processes. Its initial value is $\perp$, a value that cannot be proposed by the processes. Each process p_i uses two auxiliary local variables: val_i which contains a proposed value, and a Boolean b_i.

Algorithm 1.5 Wait-free consensus in the system model $\mathcal{CARW}_{n,t}[\text{LL/SC}]$

```
operation propose(v_i) is              % issued by p_i
(1)      val_i ← VAL.LL();
(2)      if (val_i ≠ ⊥)
(3)         then return(val_i)
(4)         else b_i ← VAL.SC();
(5)              if b_i then return(v_i)
(6)                 else val_i ← VAL.LL();
(7)                      return(val_i)
(8)              end if
(9)      end if
end of operation.
```

Building wait-free consensus in $\mathcal{CARW}_{n,t}[\text{Compare\&swap}]$ The atomic operation Compare&swap() has two input parameters called *old* and *new*.[7] Its behavior can be de-

---

[7] The theoretical power of Compare&swap() has been investigated in [19].

scribed by the atomic execution of the following sequence of statements atomically applied to a register X.

> **operation** X.Compare&swap(old, new) **is**
> $prev \leftarrow X$;
>   **if** $(X = old)$ **then** $X \leftarrow new$ **end if**;
>   return($prev$)
> **end of operation**.

Algorithm 1.6 builds a consensus object from a compare&swap register CS initialized to $\perp$ (a default value that cannot be proposed by the processes to the consensus object). Each process p_i has an auxiliary variable aux_i. When a process proposes a value v to the consensus object, it first invokes CS.Compare&swap($\perp, v$) (line 1). If it obtains $\perp$, it decides the value it proposes (line 2). Otherwise, it decides the value returned from the compare&swap register (line 3).

Algorithm 1.6 Wait-free consensus in the system model $\mathcal{CARW}_{n,t}$[Compare&swap]

> **operation** C.propose(v) **is**   % issued by p_i
> (1) $aux_i \leftarrow CS$.compare&swap($\perp, v$);
> (2)   **case** $aux_i = \perp$ **then** return(v)
> (3) $aux_i \neq \perp$ **then** return(aux_i)
> (4)   **end case**
> **end of operation**.

1.5.4 A SIMPLE WAIT-FREE CONSENSUS-BASED UNIVERSAL CONSTRUCTION

Algorithm 1.7 describes a simple wait-free consensus-based universal construction. This construction, proposed in [62], is inspired from the state machine replication paradigm [91] and the consensus-based total order broadcast algorithm presented in [35]. The reader will find a proof of it in [116]. Let O be the object that is built. As in Section 1.2, its sequential behavior is defined by a deterministic transition function $\delta()$.

Local variables at process p_i   Each process p_i manages the following local variables.

- $state_i$ contains a local copy of the object O that is built, as currently known by p_i.

- $sn_i[1..n]$ is array such that $sn_i[j]$ denotes the sequence number of the last operation on O issued by p_j locally applied to $state_i$.

- The local variables $done_i$, res_i, $prop_i$, k_i, and $list_i$, are auxiliary variables whose meaning is clear from the context; $list_i$ is a list of pairs of (operation, process identity); $|list_i|$ is its size, and $list_i[r]$ is its r-th element; hence, $list_i[r].op$ is an object operation and $list_i[r].proc$ is the process that issued it.

Algorithm 1.7 Wait-free universal construction in the model $\mathcal{CARW}_{n,t}[\text{CONS}]$

```
when pᵢ invokes op(inᵢ) do
(1)     doneᵢ ← false;
(2)     BOARD[i] ← ⟨op(inᵢ), snᵢ[i] + 1⟩;
(3)     wait (doneᵢ);
(4)     return(resᵢ)
end of invocation.

Underlying local task T is    % running in the background %
(5)     while (true) do
(6)         propᵢ ← ε;  % empty list %
(7)         for j ∈ {1,…,n} do
(8)             if (BOARD[j].sn > snᵢ[j]) then
(9)                 append (BOARD[j].op, j) to propᵢ
(10)            end if
(11)        end for;
(12)        if (propᵢ ≠ ε) then
(13)            kᵢ ← kᵢ + 1;
(14)            listᵢ ← CONS[kᵢ].propose(propᵢ);
(15)            for r = 1 to |listᵢ| do
(16)                ⟨stateᵢ, resᵢ⟩ ← δ(stateᵢ, listᵢ[r].op);
(17)                let j = listᵢ[r].proc; snᵢ[j] ← snᵢ[j] + 1;
(18)                if (i = j) then doneᵢ ← true end if
(19)            end for
(20)        end if
(21)    end while
end of task.
```

Shared registers and consensus objects implementing the object O   The shared memory contains the following objects.

- An array $BOARD[1..n]$ of single-writer multi-reader atomic registers. Each entry is a pair such that the pair $\langle BOARD[j].op, BOARD[j].sn \rangle$ contains the last operation issued by p_j and its sequence number. Each $BOARD[j]$ is initialized to $\langle \perp, 0 \rangle$.
- An unbounded array $CONS[1..]$ of consensus objects.

Process behavior   When a process p_i invokes an operation $\text{op}(in)$ on O, it registers it and its associated sequence number in $BOARD[i]$ (line 3). Then, it waits until the operation has been executed, and returns its result (line 4).

The array $BOARD$ constitutes the helping mechanism used by the background task[8] of each process p_i. This task is made up two parts, which are repeated forever. First, p_i build a proposal

---

[8]Such a task is a *thread*. It has not to be confused with the formal notion of a *distributed task* defined in Chapter 3.

$prop_i$, which includes the last operations (at most one per process) not yet applied to the object O, from its local point of view (lines 6–11 and predicate of line 8). Then, if the sequence $prop_i$ is not empty, p_i proposes it to the next consensus instance $CONS[k_i]$ line 14). The resulting value $list_i$ is a sequence of operations proposed by a process to this consensus instance. Process p_i then applies this sequence of operations to its local copy $state_i$ of O (line 16), and updates accordingly its local array sn_i (line 17). If the operation that was applied is its own operation, p_i sets the Boolean $done_i$ to true (line 18), which will terminate its current invocation (line 3).

Bounded wait-freedom vs. unbounded wait-freedom   This construction ensures that the operations issued by the processes are wait-free, but does not guarantee that they are bounded-wait-free, namely, the number of steps (accesses to the shared memory) executed before an operation terminates is finite but not bounded. Consider a process p_i that issues an operation op(), while $k1$ is the value of k_i and let $k2 = k1 + \alpha$ be such that op() is output by the consensus instance $CONS[k2]$. The task T of p_i must execute α times lines 6–20 in order to catch up the consensus instance $CONS[k2]$ and return the result produced by op(). It is easy to see that the quantity $(k2 - k1)$ is always finite but cannot be bounded.

A bounded construction is described in [66]. Instead of requiring each process to manage a local copy of the object, O is kept in shared memory and is represented by a list of records including an operation, the resulting state, the result produced by this operation, and a consensus object whose value is a pointer to the next record. The last record defines the current value of the object.

1.6   GENERALIZING UNIVERSALITY

1.6.1   UNIVERSAL CONSTRUCTION "1 AMONG k"

k-**Set agreement** k-Set agreement (k-SA) was introduced by S. Chaudhuri [37]. It is a simple generalization of consensus. It is defined by the same validity and termination properties, and a weaker agreement property, namely, at most k different values can be decided by the processes. Hence, 1-set agreement is consensus. It is shown in [22, 75, 128] that it is impossible to build a k-set agreement object in $\mathcal{CARW}_{n,t}[\emptyset]$ when k or more processes may crash.

k-**Simultaneous consensus** k-Simultaneous consensus (k-SC) was introduced in [4]. As consensus and k-SA, a k-SC object is a one-shot object that provides the processes with a single operation denoted propose(). This operation takes an input parameter a vector of size k, whose each entry contains a value, and returns a pair $\langle x, v \rangle$. The input vector contains "proposed" values, and if $\langle x, v \rangle$ is the pair returned to the invoking process, this process "decides v, and this decision is associated with the consensus instance x", $1 \leq x \leq k$.

More precisely, the behavior of a k-SC object is defined by the following properties.

- Termination. If a correct process invokes propose(), it decides a pair $\langle x, v \rangle$.

- Validity. If a process p_i decides the pair $\langle x, v \rangle$, we have $1 \le x \le k$, and the value v was proposed by a process in the entry x of its input vector parameter.

- Agreement. Let p_i be a process that decides the pair $\langle x, v \rangle$, and p_j be a process that decides the pair $\langle y, w \rangle$. We have $(x = y) \Rightarrow (v = w)$.

It is shown in [4] that k-SA and k-SC have the same computational power in the sense that a k-SA object can be built in $\mathcal{CARW}_{n,t}[k\text{-SC}]$, and a k-SC object can be built in $\mathcal{CARW}_{n,t}[k\text{-SA}]$. This equivalence is no longer true in asynchronous crash-prone message-passing systems, where k-SC is stronger than k-SA [26, 123].

Let $in_i[1..k]$ be the input parameter of a process p_i. An easy implementation of k-SC in $\mathcal{CARW}_{n,t}[\emptyset]$ enriched with k consensus objects $CONS[1..k]$ is as follows. For each x, $1 \le x \le k$, and in parallel, a process p_i proposes $in_i[x]$ to the consensus object $CONS[x]$. Let $CONS[y]$ be the first consensus object which returns a value v to p_i. Process p_i decides then the pair $\langle y, v \rangle$.

The notion of k-universality   E. Gafni and R. Guerraoui investigated in [54] the following question: what does happen if, instead of consensus objects, we use k-SA (or equivalently k-SC) objects to design a universal construction?

They showed that it is then possible to design what they called a *k-universal construction*. Such a construction considers k objects (instead of only one) and guarantees that at least one of these objects progresses forever. Algorithm 1.9 describes the k-universal construction introduced in [54]. This construction relies on k-SC objects and adopt-commit (AC) objects.

The adopt-commit object   This object, introduced by E. Gafni in [52], is a one-shot object which provides the processes with a single operation denoted propose(), which takes a value as input parameter and returns a pair composed of a tag and a value. Its behavior is defined by the following properties.

- Validity.

    - Result domain. Any returned pair $\langle tag, v \rangle$ is such that (a) v has been proposed by a process and (b) $tag \in \{\texttt{commit}, \texttt{adopt}\}$.

    - No-conflicting values. If a process p_i invokes propose(v) and returns before any other process p_j has invoked propose(w) with $w \ne v$, only the pair $\langle \texttt{commit}, v \rangle$ can be returned.

- Agreement. If a process returns $\langle \texttt{commit}, v \rangle$, only the pairs $\langle \texttt{commit}, v \rangle$ or $\langle \texttt{adopt}, v \rangle$ can be returned by the other processes.

- Termination. An invocation of propose() by a correct process always terminates.

It follows from the "no-conflicting values" property that, if a single value v is proposed, only the pair $\langle \texttt{commit}, v \rangle$ can be returned.

Algorithm 1.8 describes an implementation of the operation propose() of an adopt-commit object. It uses two underlying arrays made up of n single-writer multi-reader registers, AA and BB (only p_i can write the entries $AA[i]$ and $BB[i]$). Each array is initialized to $[\bot, \ldots, \bot]$ ($\bot$ is a value that cannot be proposed by the processes).

Let the operation XX.collect() (where XX stands for AA or BB) be an asynchronous read of the entries of the array XX and returns the set of values that have been written in XX. Each process p_i has two local variables aa_i and bb_i. The algorithm is made up of two communication phases (each involving an array) followed by a "return" phase.

- During the first communication phase, a process p_i first deposits into $AA[i]$ the value v_i it proposes (line 1) and then reads asynchronously the values proposed by the other processes (line 2).

- Then p_i executes the second communication phase. If it has seen a single value $v \neq \bot$ in the array $AA[1..n]$, p_i writes the pair $\langle single, v \rangle$ into $BB[i]$, otherwise it writes $\langle several, v_i \rangle$ (line 3).

  After having informed the other processes of what it has seen, p_i terminates the second communication phase by reading asynchronously the array $BB[1..n]$ (line 4).

- Finally, p_i computes the final value it returns as the result of its invocation of propose (v_i):

  - If a single proposed value v was seen by the processes that (to p_i's knowledge) have written into $BB[1..n]$ (those processes have consequently terminated the second communication phase), p_i commits the value v by returning the pair $\langle commit, v \rangle$ (line 5).
  - If the set of pairs read by p_i from $BB[1..n]$ contains several pairs and one of them is $\langle single, v \rangle$, p_i adopts v by returning $\langle adopt, v \rangle$.
  - Otherwise, p_i has not read $\langle single, v \rangle$ from $BB[1..n]$. In that case, it simply returns the pair $\langle adopt, v_i \rangle$.

Proofs of this algorithm can be found in [52, 116].

A non-blocking k-universal construction The construction is described by Algorithm 1.9 which considers the model $\mathcal{CARW}_{n,t}[\text{KSC}]$ ($\mathcal{CARW}_{n,t}[\emptyset]$ enriched with KSC objects). We have seen that adopt-commit objects can be implemented in $\mathcal{CARW}_{n,t}[\emptyset]$). This algorithm is based on the local replication paradigm, namely, the only shared objects are the control objects $KSC[1..]$ (unbounded list of k-SC objects) and $AC[1..][1..k]$ (matrix of adopt-commit objects). Each process p_i manages a copy of every object m, denoted $state_i[m]$, which contains the last state of m as known by p_i. The invocation by p_i of $\delta(state_i[m], \text{op})$ applies the operation op() to its local copy of object m. The construction consists in an infinite sequence of asynchronous rounds, locally denoted r_i at process p_i.

Algorithm 1.8 Wait-free adopt_commit object in the system model $\mathcal{CARW}_{n,t}[\emptyset]$

---

operation propose (v_i) **is**   % code for process p_i
(1) $AA[i] \leftarrow v_i$;
(2) $aa_i \leftarrow AA$.collect();
(3)   **if** ($aa_i = \{v\}$) **then** $BB[i] \leftarrow \langle single, v \rangle$ **else** $BB[i] \leftarrow \langle several, v_i \rangle$ **end if**;
(4) $bb_i \leftarrow BB$.collect();
(5)   **case** $bb_i = \{\langle single, v \rangle\}$ **then** return($\langle commit, v \rangle$)
(6) $bb_i = \{\langle single, v \rangle, \langle several, v' \rangle, ...\}$ **then** return($\langle adopt, \quad v \rangle$)
(7) $\langle single, v \rangle \notin bb_i$ **then** return($\langle adopt, \quad v_i \rangle$)
(8)   **end case**
end of operation.

Each process manages the following local data structures.

- For each object m, $my\_list_i[m]$ defines the list of operations that p_i wants to apply to the object m. Moreover, $my\_list_i[m]$.first() sets the read head to point to the first element of this list and returns its value; $my\_list_i[m]$.current() returns the operation under the read head; finally, $my\_list_i[m]$.next() advances the read head before returning the operation pointed to by the read head.

- For each object m, $oper_i[m]$, $ac\_op_i[m]$ are local variables which contain operations that p_i wants to apply object m (this list can be defined dynamically according to the algorithm executed by p_i); $tag_i[m]$ is used to contain a tag returned by an adopt-commit object concerning the object m.

Process behavior   A process p_i first initializes its round number, and the local copy of each object. The array $oper_i[1..k]$ is such that $oper_i[m]$ contains the next operation that p_i wants to apply to m. When this is done, it enters an infinite loop, which constitutes the core of the construction. To simplify the presentation, and without loss of generality, we consider that all object operations are different (this can be easily realized with sequence numbers and process identities). Moreover, we also do not consider the result returned by each operation.

After it has increased its round number, a process p_i invokes the k-simultaneous consensus object $KSC[r]$ to which it proposes the operation vector $oper_i[1..n]$, and from which it obtains the pair denoted $\langle obj, op \rangle$; op is an operation proposed by some process for the object obj (line 2). Process p_i then invokes the adopt-commit object $AC[r][obj]$ to which it proposes the operation op output by $KSC[r]$ for the object obj (line 3). Finally, for all the other objects $m \neq obj$, p_i invokes the adopt-commit object $AC[r][m]$ to which it proposes $oper_i[m]$ (line 4). As already indicated, the tags and the operations defined by the vector of pairs output by the adopt-commit objects $AC[r][1..k]$ are saved in the vectors $tag_i[1..k]$ and $ac\_op_i[1..k]$, respectively. The aim of these lines, realized by the objects $KSC[r]$ and $AC[r][1..m]$, is to implement a filtering mechanism such that (a) for each object, at most one operation can be be committed, and (b) there is at least

Algorithm 1.9 Non-blocking k-universal construction in the model $\mathcal{CARW}_{n,t}[KSC]$

$r_i \leftarrow 0;$ % code of p_i
for each $m \in \{1, ..., k\}$ **do**
        $state_i[m] \leftarrow$ initial state of the object m; $oper_i[m] \leftarrow my\_list_i[m].\text{first}()$
end for.

repeat forever
(1) $r_i \leftarrow r_i + 1;$
(2) $\langle obj, op \rangle \leftarrow KSC[r_i].\text{propose}(oper_i[1..k]);$
(3) $(tag_i[obj], ac\_op_i obj]) \leftarrow AC[r_i][obj].\text{propose}(op);$
(4)   **for each** $m \in \{1, ..., k\} \setminus \{obj\}$ **do**
                 $(tag_i[m], ac\_op_i[m]) \leftarrow AC[r_i][m].\text{propose}(oper_i[m])$ **end for**;
(5)   **for each** $m \in \{1, ..., k\}$ **do**
(6)   **if** $(ac\_op_i[m]$ is marked "to_be_executed_after" $oper_i[m])$
(7)   **then** $state_i[m].\delta(state_i[m], oper_i[m])$
(8)   **end if**;
(9)   **if** $(oper_i[m]$ is not marked "to_be_executed_after" $ac\_op_i[m])$
(10)   **then** **if** $(tag_i[m] = \text{adopt})$
(11)   **then** $oper_i[m] \leftarrow ac\_op_i[m]$
(12)   **else** $state_i[m] \leftarrow \delta(state_i[m], ac\_op_i[m]);$ % $tag_i[m] = \text{commit}$ %
(13)   **if** $ac\_op_i[m] = my\_list_i[m].\text{current}()$
(14)   **then** $oper_i[m] \leftarrow my\_list_i[m].\text{next}()$
(15)   **else** $oper_i[m] \leftarrow my\_list_i[m].\text{current}()$
(16)   **end if**;
(17)   mark $oper_i[m]$ "to_be_executed_after" $ac\_op_i[m]$
(18)   **end if**
(19)   **end if**
(20)   **end for**
end repeat.

one object for which an operation is committed at some process. This filtering mechanism is explained separately below.

After the execution lines 2–4, for $1 \le m \le k$, $\langle tag_i[m], ac\_op_i[m] \rangle$ contains the operation that p_i has to consider for the object m. For each of them it does the following. First, if $ac\_op_i[m]$ is marked "to be executed after" $oper_i[m]$, p_i applies $oper_i[m]$ to $state_i[m]$ (lines 6–8). Then, the predicate of line 9 ensures that no operation invocation is applied twice on the same object (this line is missing in [54]). If $tag_i[m] = \text{adopt}$, p_i adopts $ac\_op_i[m]$ as its next proposal for the object m (lines 10–11). Otherwise, $tag_i[m] = \text{commit}$. In this case p_i first applies $ac\_op_i[m]$ to its local copy $state_i[m]$ (line 12). Then, if $ac\_op_i[m]$ was an operation it has issued, p_i computes its next operation $oper_i[m]$ on the object m (lines 13–16).

As explained in [54], the use of a naive strategy to update local copies of the objects, makes possible the following bad scenario. During a round r, a process p_1 executes an operation op1 on its copy of the object $m1$, while a process p_2 executes a operation op2 on a different object $m2$. Then, during round $r + 1$, p_1 executes a operation op3 on the object $m2$ without having executed first op2 on its copy of $m2$. This bad behavior is prevented from occurring by a combined used

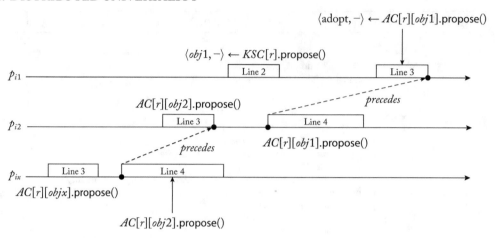

Figure 1.7: Net effect of the k-SC and CA objects used at lines 2–4 of round r.

of adopt-commit objects and an appropriate marking mechanism. When a process p_i applies an operation op() to its local copy of an object m, it has necessarily received the pair $\langle$commit, op()$\rangle$ from the adopt-commit object associated with the current round, and consequently the other processes have received $\langle$commit, op()$\rangle$ or $\langle$adopt, op()$\rangle$. The process p_i attaches then to its next operation for the object m (which is denoted $oper_i[m]$) the indication that $oper_i[m]$ has to be applied to m after op() so that no process executes $oper_i[m]$ without having previously executed op(). Hence, to prevent the bad behavior previously described, a process p_i attaches to $oper_i[m]$ (line 17) the fact that this operation cannot be applied to any copy of the object m before the operation $ac\_op_i[m]$.

As already indicated, this k-universal construction ensures that at least one process progresses forever (non-blocking progress condition), and at least one object progresses forever.

Why at least one object operation is committed at every round   It was claimed above that the "filtering mechanism" realized by lines 2–4 ensures that at least one operation is committed at every round. We prove here this claim. Figure 1.7 illustrates the associated reasoning.

After (line 2) a process p_{i1} obtained a pair $\langle obj1, op1 \rangle$ from its invocation $KSC[r]$.propose($oper_i[1..k]$), it invokes $AC[r][obj1]$.propose($op1$) at line 3, and only then it invokes $AC[r][obj]$.propose($op1$) for each object $obj \neq obj1$ at line 4. If its invocation of $AC[r][obj1]$.propose($op1$) at line 3 returns $\langle$commit, $-\rangle$, the claim follows.

Hence, let us assume that the invocation of $AC[r][obj1]$.propose($op1$) by p_{i1} returns $\langle$abort, $-\rangle$. It follows from the "non-conflicting" property of the AC object $AC[r][obj1]$ that another process p_{i2} has necessarily invoked the operation $AC[r][obj1]$.propose(op') with $op' \neq op1$; moreover, this invocation by p_{i2} was issued at line 4 (if both p_{i1} and p_{i2} had invoked $AC[r][obj1]$.propose() at line 3, due to agreement property of $AC[r][obj1]$, they would have obtained the same pair from this object at line 3, and consequently p_{i2} could not have prevented p_{i1} from obtaining $\langle \text{commit}, - \rangle$ from the AC object $AC[r][obj1]$ at line 3). If follows that p_{i2} started line 4 before p_{i1} terminated line 3. The invocation by p_{i2} at line 3 of $AC[r][-]$ involved some object $obj2$ obtained by p_{i2} at line 2, and we necessarily have $obj2 \neq obj1$).

If the invocation of $AC[r][obj2]$.propose() returns $\langle \text{commit}, - \rangle$, the claim follows. Otherwise, due to the agreement property of $AC[r][obj2]$, there is a process p_{i3}, different from p_{i1} and p_{i2}, such that the execution pattern between $p_{i3} \neq p_{i2}$ is the same as the previous pattern between $p_{i2} \neq p_{i1}$, etc. The claim then follows by induction and the fact that there is finite number of processes.

1.6.2   ULTIMATE UNIVERSAL CONSTRUCTION "ℓ AMONG k"

The previous NB-compliant k-universal construction ensures that at least one object progresses forever, and one process progresses forever. Hence, the natural question: Is it possible to design a universal construction in which at least ℓ objects progress forever, where $1 \leq \ell \leq k$, and all correct processes progress forever (wait-freedom progress condition).

Such a very general universal construction was proposed by M. Raynal, J. Stainer, and G. Taubenfeld in [124]. It rests on an extension of the k-SC object called (k, ℓ)-simultaneous consensus.

(k, ℓ)-**Simultaneous consensus**   Let $\ell \in \{1, \ldots, k\}$. A (k, ℓ)-SC object is a k-SC object (see Section 1.6.1) where instead of a single pair $\langle x, v \rangle$, the operation propose() returns a set of exactly ℓ pairs $\{\langle x_1, v_1 \rangle, \ldots, \langle x_\ell, v_\ell \rangle\}$, such that all the pairs differ in their first component.

It is easy to see that $(k, 1)$-SC object is a k-SC object (and consequently a k-SA object). It is also easy to see that a (k, k)-SC object is a consensus object. For $k > 1$, a (k, ℓ)-SC object is weaker than a $(k, \ell + 1)$-SC object.

(k, ℓ)-**Universal construction**   The (k, ℓ)-universal construction presented in [124] borrows lines 1–4 of Algorithm 1.9, in which k-SC objects are replaced by (k, ℓ)-SC objects. All the rest of the construction, which is built incrementally, is based on a different approach. A nonblocking k-universal construction is first described, and then enriched step by step to obtain the final WF-compliant (k, ℓ)-universal construction. Its noteworthy features are the following.

- On the object side. At least ℓ among the k objects progress forever, $1 \leq \ell \leq k$. This means that an infinite number of operations is applied to each of these ℓ objects. This set of ℓ objects is not predetermined, and depends on the execution.

- On the process side. The progress condition associated with processes is wait-freedom. That is, a process that does not crash executes an infinite number of operations on each object that progresses forever.

- An object stops progressing when no more operations are applied to it. The construction guarantees that, when an object stops progressing, all its copies stop in the same state (at the non-crashed processes).

- The construction is *contention-aware*. This means that the overhead introduced by using operations on memory locations other than atomic read/write registers is eliminated when there is no contention during the execution of an object operation. In the absence of contention, a process completes its operations by accessing only read/write registers.

- The construction is *generous* with respect to *obstruction-freedom*. This means that each process is able to complete its pending operations on all the k objects each time all the other processes hold still long enough. That is, if once and again all the processes except one hold still long enough, then all the k objects, and not just ℓ objects, are guaranteed to always progress.

- Last but least, it is shown in [124] that (k, ℓ)-simultaneous consensus objects are necessary and sufficient to implement a (k, ℓ)-universal construction, i.e., to ensure that at least ℓ among k objects progress forever while guaranteeing the wait-freedom progress condition to the processes. Relations between $(k, k - p)$-SC objects and $(p + 1)$-set agreement objects for $0 \leq p < k$ are also investigated in [124].

1.7 UNIVERSAL CONSTRUCTION vs. SOFTWARE TRANSACTIONAL MEMORY

A universal construction concerns the distributed implementation of concurrent objects defined by a sequential specification. The concept of a *software transactional memory* (STM), introduced in [70], and later refined in [131], is different. Its aim is to provide the programmers with a language construct (called *transaction*) that discharges them from the management of synchronization issues. In this way, a programmer can concentrate his efforts on which parts of processes have to be executed atomically and not on the way atomicity is realized. This last issue is then the job of the underlying STM system. Among others, main differences between universal constructions and STM systems are the following.

- Object operations are defined *a priori* (statically), and the universal construction knows them. Differently, the transactions are defined dynamically, and the STM system has no priori knowledge of their content and their effects.

  Let us also notice that, despite the fact they have the same name, database transactions [60] and STM transactions are not the same. Database transactions are constrained in the sense that they are the result of queries expressed in a given formalism. Differently, STM transactions can be any piece of code produced by a programmer, which must be executed atomically. Moreover, usually the code of the STM transactions is not known by the STM system.

• The consistency condition of concurrent objects (captured at run-time by linearizability [76]) and the consistency conditions of STM systems (e.g., opacity [61], virtual world consistency [82], or TMS1 [44]) are different. Among other points, this comes from the fact that any two transactions are *a priori* independent [39].

• Due to their very nature, universal constructions consider failure-prone systems. Differently, some STMs address failure-free systems while others address failure-prone systems.

1.8   CONCLUSION

The aim of this chapter was to be a guided visit to universal constructions in asynchronous crash-prone systems, where the processes communicate through a shared memory. As announced in the introduction, its ambition was to be a relatively easy way to understand the notion of a "universal construction" and the important concepts and objects which constitute the foundations on which rely the algorithms building universal constructions.

To this end, this chapter has first presented a simple construction based on hardware operations on memory locations, namely the LL/SC pair of operations. It then moved from hardware-provided operations to agreement objects, and presented a simple consensus-based universal construction. Finally, the chapter considered the case where the aim is not to address the construction of a single object, but the coordinated construction of several objects. It is important to realize that, if not all the objects which are built are required to progress forever, hardware operations such as LL/SC or Compare&swap, are stronger than necessary to build universal constructions.

As a final remark, let us notice that OB-compliant (obstruction-free) universal constructions do not require to enrich the system with the additional computational power provided by hardware atomic operations such as LL/SC or agreement objects, i.e., they can be done in the basic system model $\mathcal{CARW}[\emptyset]$. This remains true even if the processes are anonymous. The algorithms presented in [25] build both an OB-compliant consensus object and an OB-compliant repeated consensus object in the system model $\mathcal{CARW}[\emptyset]$ weakened by the fact that processes are anonymous with only n read/write atomic registers, which is conjectured to be optimal (it is proved in [141] that at least $(n-1)$ registers are necessary).

CHAPTER 2

Consensus Numbers and Beyond

Since its introduction by M. Herlihy in 1991, the *consensus number* notion has become central to capture and understand the agreement and synchronization power of objects in the presence of asynchrony and any number of process crashes. This notion has now become fundamental in shared memory systems, when one is interested in the design of universal constructions for high level objects defined by a sequential specification.

The aim of this chapter is to be a guided tour in the wonderful land of consensus numbers. In addition to more ancient results, it also presents recent results related to the existence of an infinity of objects—of increasing synchronization/agreement power—at each level of the consensus hierarchy.

Keywords: Agreement, Asynchronous read/write system, Atomic operation, Concurrent object, Consensus, Consensus hierarchy, Crash failure, Deterministic object, Distributed computability, Progress condition, Sequential specification, k-Set agreement, Universal construction, Wait-freedom.

2.1   PRELIMINARIES

Computability power   The fundamental notions of wait-freedom and universal construction have been presented in the previous chapter. It has been shown in [66, 97] that the design of a wait-free universal construction is impossible in asynchronous read/write systems (model $\mathcal{CARW}_{n,t}[\emptyset]$) when any number of processes may crash.[1] This means that asynchronous failure-prone systems need to be enriched with additional objects whose *computability power* is strictly stronger than the one of atomic read/write registers [119].[2] The objects that, together with any number of read/write registers, allow to build a wait-free universal construction are said to be *universal*. As shown in the previous chapter, the *consensus* object is universal, as are LL/SC and Compare&swap registers.

---

[1]The first proof of such an impossibility was done in the context of asynchronous message-passing systems where even a single process may crash [50].

[2]Given a computing model (for example, the finite state automaton model or the Turing machine model in sequential computing), the notion of *computability power* is on what can and what cannot be computed in this model. Differently, given a computing model, the notion of *computing power* refers to efficiency.

Content of the chapter   After a short reminder on the consensus object,[3] Section 2.2 introduces the notion of consensus number [66]. Section 2.3 shows that there is an infinity of objects whose consensus number is 1, while their computability power is strictly increasing [40].

Section 2.4 shows that for any $x \geq 2$, there is an infinity of objects whose consensus number is x, while their computability power is strictly increasing [3]. Historically, the case $x \geq 2$ was investigated before the case $x = 1$ (2016 and 2018, respectively). The parlance "life beyond consensus" was introduced in [3].

2.2   THE CONSENSUS HIERARCHY

2.2.1   TWO AGREEMENT OBJECTS

Consensus   As already indicated, the notion of a *universal* object with respect to fault-tolerance was introduced by M. Herlihy [66]. An object type T is *universal* if it is possible to wait-free implement any object (defined by a sequential specification) in the asynchronous read/write model, where any number of processes may crash, enriched with any number of objects of type T. An algorithm providing such an implementation is called a *universal construction*. It is shown in [66] that *consensus* objects are universal. These objects, introduced in [107], allow the processes to propose values and agree on one of them. More precisely, such an object provides the processes with a single operation, denoted propose(), that a process can invoke only once. This operation returns a value to the invoking process. When p_i invokes propose(v_i) we say that it "proposes the value v_i," and if v is the returned value we say that it "decides v." The consensus object is defined by the three following properties:

- Validity. The value decided by a process was proposed by a process.

- Agreement. No two processes decide different values.

- Termination. If a correct process invokes propose(), it decides a value.

Termination states that if a correct process invokes propose(), it decides a value whatever the behavior of the other processes (wait-freedom progress condition). Validity connects the output to the inputs, while Agreement states that the processes cannot decide differently. A sequence of consensus objects is used in the following way in a universal construction. According to its current view of the operations invoked on (and not yet applied to) the object O of type T that is built, each process proposes to the next consensus instance a sequence of operations to be applied to O, and the winning sequence is actually applied. A helping mechanism [33, 116] is used to ensure that all the operations on O (at least by the processes that do not crash) are eventually applied to O.

---

[3]This is to make the reading of this chapter as autonomous as possible from the content of the previous chapter.

k-**Set agreement**   A k-*set agreement* object (in short k-SA) is a simple an natural weakening of the consensus object [37]. It has the same Validity and Termination properties, but a weaker Agreement property, namely:

- Agreement. At most k different values are decided.

Hence, consensus is 1-set agreement. It is shown in [22, 75, 128] that it is impossible to implement k-set agreement on top of read/write registers, in the presence of asynchrony and any number of process crashes.

   k-Set agreement where $k = n - 1$ is called *set agreement*. It is worth noting that, if all the processes propose different values (which is not know in advance), consensus consists in selecting a single value while set-agreement consists in eliminating a single value. If the identity of the invoking process is part of the value it proposes, consensus selects one process, while set-agreement eliminates one of them.

2.2.2   THE CONSENSUS HIERARCHY

Consensus numbers and consensus hierarchy   The concept of *consensus number* was introduced by M. Herlihy [66]. The consensus number of an object type T (denoted CN(T) in the following) is the greatest positive integer n such that a consensus object can be built in an asynchronous crash-prone n-process system from any number of atomic read/write registers and any number of objects of type T. If there is no such finite n, the consensus number of T is $+\infty$. Hence, a type T such that CN(T) $\geq n$ is universal in a system of n (or less) processes.

   It appears that the consensus numbers define an infinite hierarchy (also called "Herlihy's hierarchy") in which atomic read/write registers have consensus number 1, object types such as Test&Set, Fetch&Add, and Swap, have consensus number 2, etc., until object types such as Compare&Swap, Linked Load/Store Conditional (and a few others) that have consensus number $+\infty$. In between, read/write registers provided with m-assignment[4] with $m > 1$ have consensus number $(2m - 2)$.

Notations   The following notations are used in this chapter.

- For $x \geq 1$, $\mathcal{CN}(x)$ denotes the set all the object types T whose such that CN(T) = x.

- If an object type has a single operation op(), CN(op) denotes its consensus number.

- If $T1$ and $T2$ are two object types such that CN($T1$) $<$ CN($T2$), we also write $T1 <$ $T2$.

- If $CN(T) = x$ and O is an object of type T, we say that O is an x-consensus object (i.e., O allows consensus to be solved in an x-process system, but not in an $(x + 1)$-process system).

---

[4]Such an assignment updates atomically m read/write registers. It is sometimes written $X_1, X_2, \ldots, X_m \leftarrow v_1, \ldots, v_m$ where the X_i are the registers, and each v_i the value assigned to X_i.

- Let T be an object type. $T < \mathcal{CN}(x)$ means that $CN(T) < x$, and similarly for $T > \mathcal{CN}(x)$.

- Let $A < B$ denote the fact that object A can be built in an n-process system where the processes communicate through read/write registers and objects B, while object B cannot be built from object A and read/write registers.

An object family covering the whole consensus hierarchy The object named k-*sliding read/write register* (in short RW_k) was introduced in [103] (a similar object was independently introduced in [47]). It is a natural generalization of an atomic read/write register, which corresponds to the case $k = 1$. Let $KREG$ be such an object. It can be seen as a sequence of values, accessed by two atomic operations denoted $KREG$.write() and $KREG$.read().

The invocation of $KREG$.write(v) by a process adds the value v at the end of the sequence $KREG$, while an invocation of $KREG$.read() returns the ordered sequence of the last k written values (if only $x < k$ values have been written, the default value $\bot$ replaces each of the $(k - x)$ missing values).

Hence, conceptually, an RW_k object is a sequence containing all the values that have been written (in their atomicity-defined writing order), and whose each read operation returns the k values that have been written just before it, according to the atomicity order. As already indicated, it is easy to see that, for $k = 1$, RW_k is a classical atomic read/write register. For $k = +\infty$, each read operation returns the whole sequence of values written so far. Let us notice that RW_∞ is nothing else than a ledger object [120].

It is shown in [103] that the consensus number of RW_k is k. Hence, from a computability point of view we have

$$\text{R/W registers} = RW_1 < RW_2 < \cdots < RW_k < RW_{k+1} < \cdots < RW_\infty.$$

2.2.3   A GLANCE INSIDE THE CONSENSUS NUMBER LAND

Multiplicative power of consensus numbers The notion named *multiplicative power of consensus numbers* was introduced in [80]. It considers system models made up of n processes prone to up to t crashes, and where the processes communicate by accessing read/write atomic registers and x-consensus objects (with $x \leq t < n$). Let $ASM(n, t, x)$ denote such a system model. While the BG simulation [22] (see Chapter 4) shows that the models $ASM(n, t, 1)$ and $ASM(t + 1, t, 1)$ are equivalent from a (colorless task) computability power point of view, the work presented in [80] focuses on the pair (t, x) of the system model parameters. Its main result is the following: the system models $ASM(n_1, t_1, x_1)$ and $ASM(n_2, t_2, x_2)$ have the same computability power if and only if $\lfloor \frac{t_1}{x_1} \rfloor = \lfloor \frac{t_2}{x_2} \rfloor$. This contribution, which complements and extends the BG simulation, shows that consensus numbers have a multiplicative power with respect to failures, namely the system models $ASM(n, t', x)$ and $ASM(n, t, 1)$ are equivalent (for colorless decision tasks) if and only if $(t \times x) \leq t' \leq (t \times x) + (x - 1)$.

Combining object types The consensus hierarchy considers that consensus must be built from read/write registers and objects of a given type T only. Hence, the question "is it possible to *combine* objects with a *small* consensus number to obtain a new object with a greater consensus number?" As an example, let us consider the two following object types $T1$ and $T2$, whose consensus number is 2 (see [47] for more developments).

- An object of type $T1$ can be read and accessed by the operation Test&set(), which returns its current value and sets it to 1 if it contained 0.

- An object of type $T2$ can be read and accessed by the operation Fetch&add2(), which returns the current value of the object, and increases it by 2.

Let us now consider an object type $T12$ which provides three operations: read(), Test&set(), and Fetch&add2(). Algorithm 2.1 (introduced in [47]) shows that a binary consensus object can be built from read/write registers and objects $T12$ in a crash-prone system of any number of processes. Binary consensus means that only the values 0 and 1 can be proposed.[5] We consequently have $CN(T12) = +\infty$.

Algorithm 2.1 A wait-free binary consensus algorithm from object type $T12$

```
operation propose(v) do                          % code for p_i
(1)      if (v = 0) then X.Fetch&add2();
(2)                  if (X is odd) then return(1) else return(0) end if
(3)          else  x ← X.Test&set();
(4)                  if (x is odd) ∨ (x = 0) then return(1) else return(0) end if
(5)      end if
end of operation.
```

The internal representation of the binary consensus object is an object X of type $T12$, initialized to 0. According to the value it proposes (0 or 1), a process executes the statements of lines 2–3 or the statements of lines 4–5. The value returned by the consensus object is sealed by the first atomic operation that is executed. It is 0 if the first operation on X is X.Fetch&add2(), and 1 if first operation on X is X.Test&set(). The reader can check that, if the first operation on X is Fetch&add2(), X becomes and remains even forever. If it is Test&set(), X becomes and remains odd forever. In the first case, only 0 can be decided, while in the second case, only 1 can be decided.

Relations linking the Test&set() object with adaptive renaming and set agreement are presented in [58].

Relaxing object operations In [130] the authors consider many classical objects (such as queues, stacks, sets) and relax the semantics of their operations in order to see if these relax-

---

[5]This is not a problem as it is possible to build a multivalued consensus object from binary consensus objects, see [116].

ations modify the consensus number of the relaxed object, and consequently are more tolerant to the net effect of asynchrony and process failures.

As an example, let us consider the well-known type Q (queue) defined the three following operations: enqueue(), which adds a value at the end of the queue, dequeue(), which returns the oldest value of the queue and suppresses it from the queue, and peek(), which returns the oldest value without modifying the content of the queue. The following relaxed queue type, denoted $Q_{a,b,c}$, was introduced and investigated in [130]. Each possible (statically defined) triple of the type parameters a, b, and c gives rise to an instance of a *relaxed* queue type, defined by the three following atomic operations:

- enqueue$_a(v)$ inserts the value v at any one of the a positions at the end of the queue,[6]

- dequeue$_b()$ returns and removes one of the values at the b positions at the end of the queue, and

- peek$_c()$ returns (without removing it) one of the values at the b positions at the end of the queue.

Whatever the operation, it returns a default value $\perp$ if the queue is empty. When the type parameter a, b, or c is equal to 0, the corresponding operation is not supported. When it is ∞ it means that the corresponding operation can add, remove/return a value at any position. It is easy to see that the object type $Q_{1,1,0}$ is the usual queue object (without peek() operation), whose consensus number is 2 [66]. Let us observe that the smaller the value of the parameter $a \geq 1$, $b \geq 1$, or $c \geq 1$, the stronger the constraint imposed by the corresponding operation. Among many others, the following results are shown in [130].

- The consensus number of $Q_{1,1,1}$ is ∞, while the consensus number of $Q_{\infty,1,1}$ is 2. This comes from the fact that enqueue$_\infty()$ allows a value to be inserted at any position, while enqueue$_1()$ imposes a very constrained order on value insertions.

- The consensus number of $Q_{1,1,2}$ is 2 (this follows from the relaxed operation peek$_2()$).

- For $a > 0$, the consensus number of $Q_{a,0,1}$ is $+\infty$.

The notion of power number of an object   *Obstruction-freedom* is a progress condition (hence, a termination property) introduced in [69]. It was later extended to k-obstruction-freedom in [138] as follows ($k = 1$ gives obstruction-freedom):

- Termination. If a set of at most k processes execute alone during a long enough time and do not crash, each of them terminates its operation.

Hence, k-obstruction-freedom states that, during long enough period during which the concurrency degree does not bypass k, the operations terminate. While wait-freedom is independent

---

[6]The position of an item (value) in a queue is the number of items that precede it plus 1.

of both the concurrency pattern and the failure pattern, obstruction-freedom depend on them. More general *asymmetric* progress conditions have been introduced in [84]. The computational structure of progress conditions is investigated in [138].

The notion of the *power number* of an object type T (denoted $PN(T)$) was introduced in [138]. It is the largest integer k such that it is possible to implement a k-obstruction-free consensus object for *any* number of processes, using any number of atomic read/write registers, and any number of objects of type T (the registers and the objects of type T being wait-free). If there is no such largest integer k, $PN(T) = +\infty$.

Hence, the power number of an object type T establishes a strong relation linking k-obstruction-freedom and wait-freedom, when objects of type T are used. Let us remember that $CN(T)$ is the consensus number of the objects of type T. It is shown in [138] that $CN(T) = PN(T)$.

The notion of set agreement power   As defined in [42, 55], the set agreement power of an object type T is the infinite sequence $\langle n_1, \ldots, n_k, n_{k+1}, \ldots \rangle$, such that for any ≥ 1, n_k is the greatest number of processes for which it is possible to wait-free solve k-set agreement with any number of objects of type T and read/write registers. As an example, for $n \geq 2$, the set agreement power of the $(n-1)$-consensus object type is $\langle n_1, \ldots, n_k, n_{k+1}, \ldots \rangle$, where for all $k \geq 1$, $n_k = k(n-1)$ [38].

It is shown in [34] that at each level $\ell \geq 2$ of the consensus hierarchy, there are objects that, while they have the same set agreement power, are not equivalent (i.e., at least one of them cannot implement the other). This result has been extended to deterministic objects in [36].

When there is no bound on the number of processes   In some applications, processes can be dynamically created during an execution so that there is no *a priori* fixed bound on the number of participating processes. On another side, the processes have access to memory allocation mechanism that cannot allocate infinite arrays.

Considering such a dynamic context, the wait-free Herlihy's hierarchy has been extended in [108] to cope with the previous issues. To this end, the authors subdivide the set of synchronization objects whose consensus number is infinite in nine degrees according to (i) their abilities to synchronize a set of bounded, finite or infinite, number of processes and (ii) the fact that the processes need or do not need allocate infinite arrays.

From the process crash model to the crash-recovery model   The consensus hierarchy in a crash-recovery model has first been addressed in [21]. This model assumes that a failure resets the local variables of a process to their initial values (the local variables include the program counter of the process), and preserves the state of the shared objects. It is shown in [21] that consensus remains sufficiently powerful to implement (in this model) any sequentially defined concurrent object.

The notion of *recoverable consensus* has been introduced in [59]. Such a consensus is defined by the classical Validity and Agreement properties of consensus and the following Termination property: Each time a process invokes a recoverable consensus instance, it returns a decision or crashes. This means that if a process invokes a recoverable consensus instance and, while executing it, crashes a finite number of times, it decides. It is shown in [59] that the consensus number of the Test&Set() operation (which is 2 in the crash failure model) is still 2 in the crash-recovery model if failures are simultaneous, but drops to 1 if failures are independent. As stated in [59], this captures the fact that, "when failures are simultaneous, a process recovers with more information regarding the states of other processes, than when failures are independent."

2.3   LIFE IN THE "CONSENSUS NUMBER 1" LAND

This section presents an infinite family of deterministic objects, denoted WRN_3, WRN_4, ..., WRN_k, WRN_{k+1}, etc., such that:

- none of them can be wait-free built from atomic read/write registers only,

- WRN_{k+1} can be wait-free built from WRN_k but cannot build it, and

- none of these objects can wait-free implement a 2-consensus in an n-process asynchronous crash-prone system.

It follows that this infinite countable family of objects are totally ordered by their computability power are stronger than read/write registers (whose consensus number is 1), and are weaker than all the objects whose consensus number is greater or equal to 2. The results presented in this section are due to E. Daian, G. Losa, Y. Afek, and E. Gafni [40] and concern deterministic objects. The case of non-deterministic objects, for which there are similar results, was addressed in [112].

2.3.1   THE FAMILY OF "WRITE AND READ NEXT" OBJECTS

The WRN object family (where WRN stands for *Write and Read Next*) is a generic family, in which each instance of the genericity parameter k ($k > 2$) gives rise to a specific object type denoted WRN_k.

   A WRN_k object has a single atomic operation denoted $wrn_k()$, which can be invoked at most once by a process. From an conceptual point of view, this object can be seen as an array $A[0..k-1]$ initialized to $[\bot, \ldots, \bot]$. A process p_i invokes $wrn_k(i, v)$ where $i \in \{0, \ldots, k-1\}$ and v is a value to be stored in the WRN object. The effect of the invocation of $wrn_k(i, v)$ is defined by the atomic execution of Algorithm 2.2, where it is assumed that $v \neq \bot$. The ring structure $\langle i, (i+1), \ldots, (k-1), 0, 1, \ldots, i \rangle$, and its use in the write of $A[i]$ followed by the read of $A[(i+1) \bmod k]$ is the key providing the computability power of a WRN_k object.

   It is easy to see that the object WRN_k is deterministic (namely, the value returned by $wrn_k()$ and the new value of A depend on the previous value of A and the input parameters of the $wrn_k()$ operation only).

Algorithm 2.2 The operation $\mathsf{wrn}_k(i, v)$ (invoked by p_i)

$$
\begin{aligned}
&\textbf{operation } \mathsf{wrn}_k(i, v) \textbf{ is }\quad \% \, i \in \{1, \ldots, k-1\}, v \neq \perp \\
&(1) \qquad A[i] \leftarrow v; \\
&(2) \qquad \mathsf{return}(A[(i+1) \bmod k]) \\
&\textbf{end of operation.}
\end{aligned}
$$

2.3.2   COMPUTABILITY POWER OF WRN$_k$ IN A k-PROCESS SYSTEM

This section shows that a WRN_k object ($k > 2$) cannot be built from read/write registers (and is consequently stronger than them), and cannot solve consensus for two processes in a set of k processes. To this end it shows that, for any $k > 2$, it is possible to solve $(k, k-1)$-set consensus (i.e., $(k-1)$-set consensus in a set of k processes) from a WRN_k object, and WRN_k can be built from $(k, k-1)$-set consensus and atomic read/write registers. The result then follows from the fact that $(k-1)$-set consensus cannot be wait-free solved from read/write registers [22, 75, 128], and cannot solve consensus for two processes.

From a WRN$_k$ object to $(k, k-1)$-set consensus   Algorithm 2.3 realizes such a construction. It uses an underlying object WRN_k, accessed by k processes p_0, ..., p_{k-1} (where i is the index/identity of p_i). A process p_i first invokes $WRN_k.\mathsf{wrn}_k(i, v_i)$ where v_i is the value it proposes (line 1). Hence, it writes the entry i of the underlying WRN_k object and reads its next entry, namely $(i+1) \bmod k$ (Algorithm 2.2). Then (line 2), if the value it obtains from WRN_k is different from $\perp$, it returns it. Otherwise, it returns the value v_i it proposed.

Algorithm 2.3 Operation propose(i, v_i) of $(k, k-1)$-set agreement in a k-process system

$$
\begin{aligned}
&\textbf{operation } \mathsf{propose}(i, v_i) \textbf{ is }\qquad\qquad \% \text{ code for } p_i \\
&(1) \qquad aux_i \leftarrow WRN_k.\mathsf{wrn}_k(i, v_i); \\
&(2) \qquad \textbf{if } (aux_i \neq \perp) \textbf{ then } r_i \leftarrow aux_i \textbf{ else } r_i \leftarrow v_i \textbf{ end if}; \\
&(3) \qquad \mathsf{return}(r_i) \\
&\textbf{end of operation.}
\end{aligned}
$$

Algorithm 2.3 is trivially wait-free. Let us also observe that, as the process indices are in $\{0, \ldots, (k-1)\}$ and no two processes have the same index, any entry of WRN_k can be written by a single process. Moreover, due to the content of WRN_k and line 2, it follows that only proposed values can be returned.

Let us consider any process p_j that decides. Such a process returns the value written by $p_{(j+1) \bmod k}$, or its own value v_j (when $p_{(j+1) \bmod k}$ crashed before it deposited its proposed value $v_{(j+1) \bmod k}$ in WRN_k). As the invocations of $WRN_k.\mathsf{wrn}_k()$ are atomic (i.e., they appear as if they have been executed one after the other in a real time-compliant order), it follows that the first process that invokes $WRN_k.\mathsf{wrn}_k()$ always returns its own value. Moreover, if all the processes decide, all the entries of WRN_k have been filled in, and the last process, say p_x, that executes $WRN_k.\text{wrn}_k()$, returns the value written by $p_{(x+1) \bmod k}$. Hence, the value proposed by p_x is not decided, and consequently at most $(k - 1)$ values are decided.

From $(k, k - 1)$-set consensus to a WRN_k object   This construction (described in [40]) starts from a solution to $(k, k - 1)$-set consensus, which is first transformed into a $(k, k - 1)$-strong "set election" object. This object is such that if a process p_i decides the value v_j proposed by a process p_j, then, if p_j decides, it decides also v_j (implementations are described in [22, 56]). The construction of a WRN_k object from a $(k, k - 1)$-strong set election object uses additional snapshot objects [1], the consensus number of which is 1.

What has been shown   The previous discussion has shown that, in an asynchronous k-process system, where any number of processes may crash, $(k, k - 1)$-set agreement and WRN_k objects are computationally equivalent. Hence, as the computability power of $(k, k - 1)$-set agreement is stronger than the one of read/write registers and is weaker than the one of objects whose consensus number is 2, the same follows from WRN_k objects in a k-process system.

2.3.3   WHEN THERE ARE MORE THAN k PROCESSES

Where is the difficulty   Let us now assume that there are $n > k$ processes, p_0, ..., p_{n-1}, and WRN_k objects, each being accessed by a specific set of k processes, e.g., p_{i_1}, ..., p_{i_k}. There are two cases according to the fact, for each WRN_k object, the subset of k processes that access it is statically or dynamically defined.

Whatever the case, the important issue that has to be solved comes from the fact that the k entries 0, 1, ..., $(k - 1)$ of the WRN_k object, do not necessarily correspond to the k indexes (belonging to the set $\{0, \dots, n - 1\}$) of the k processes that access the considered WRN_k object. This means that addressing issues must be solved to pair-wise associate the indexes of the k concerned processes with the k entries of a WRN_k object.

Index addressing in the static case   Let $\text{comb}(k, n)$ be the number of subsets of k elements taken from a set of $n > k$ elements. There are consequently $\text{comb}(k, n)$ possible WRN_k objects, namely an object per subset of k different processes. Let us order all these subsets from 1 to $\text{comb}(k, n)$, obtaining the subsets sbs_1, ..., $sbs_{\text{comb}(k,n)}$. Moreover, let us order the process indexes in each subset sbs_x, according to their increasing values. Finally, for each $x \in \{1, \dots, \text{comb}(k, n)\}$, let $f_x(i)$, where i is a process index belonging to sbs_x, the position of i (starting from position 0) in the ordered subset sbs_x. Hence, $f_x(i)$ is an index in $\{0, \dots, k - 1\}$, and for any two different indexes $i, j \in sbs_x$ we have $f_x(i) \neq f_x(j)$.

$(k, k - 1)$-**Set agreement in an n-process system in the static case**   A construction of a $(k, k - 1)$-set agreement object in a system of n processes, is described in Algorithm 2.4. This construction is a simple "index reduction." Let sbs_x be the set of processes that invoke the considered WRN_k object, which is consequently denoted $WRN_k[sbs_x]$. The index mapping function $f_x()$ is known by the processes in sbs_x.

Algorithm 2.4 propose(i, v_i) of $(k, k-1)$-set agreement in an n-process system (static case)

```
operation propose(i, vi) is       % code for pi, i ∈ sbsx
(1)     i' ← fx(i);
(2)     auxi ← WRNk[sbsx].wrn(i', vi);
(3)     if (auxi ≠ ⊥) then r ← auxi else ri ← vi end if;
(4)     return(ri)
end of operation.
```

Index addressing in the dynamic case   Using renaming algorithms (e.g., [23, 31]), it is possible to rename k processes whose identities belong to the set $\{0, \ldots, n-1\}$ with new k distinct identities belonging to the set $\{0, \ldots, 2k-2\}$. Hence, while Algorithm 2.3 needs k processes with distinct identities in $\{0, \ldots, k-1\}$, we have now k processes with identities in $\{0, \ldots, 2k-2\}$.

The set F of all the functions from $\{0, \ldots, 2k-2\}$ to $\{0, \ldots, k-1\}$ contains $(2k-1)^k$ functions, which can be totally ordered. Let $f_1, \ldots, f_{(2k-1)^k}$ be such a total ordering (statically known by the k concerned processes). Moreover, let us also observe that, R being the set of the new identities (dynamically obtained of the k concerned processes), there is a function $f^\star \in F$ such that $\{f^\star(i) \mid i \in R\} = \{0, \ldots, k-1\}$. Let us notice that, while F is known by all the processes, none of the k processes knows which one is $f^\star$. Let us also observe that the set F contains also functions f such that there are there are $i, j \in R$ such that $f(i) = f(j)$.

$(k, k-1)$-**Set agreement in an n-process system in the dynamic case**   A construction of a $(k, k-1)$-set agreement object in a system of n processes, is described in Algorithm 2.5. This construction uses $(2k-1)^k$ WRN_k objects, denoted $WRN_k[1..(2k-1)^k]$.

Algorithm 2.5 propose(i, v_i) of $(k, k-1)$-set agreement in an n-process system (dynamic case)

```
operation propose(i, vi) is   % code for pi, 0 ≤ i ≤ n − 1
(1)  j ← rename(i);
(2)  for ℓ from 1 to (2k − 1)k do
(3)      j' ← fℓ(j);
(4)      auxi ← WRNk[ℓ].wrn(j', vi);
(5)      if (auxi ≠ ⊥) then return(auxi) end if
(6)  end for;
(7)  return(vi)
end of operation.
```

A process p_i first invokes a renaming algorithm (line 1) from which it obtains a new name $j \in \{1, \ldots, 2k-2\}$. Then, the k processes execute a loop, in the same predefined order (namely

$\ell = 1, 2, \ldots, (2k - 1)^k$, line 2), in which p_i considers it has the identity j' as defined by $f_\ell(j)$ (line 3). Then, p_i uses the next underlying object $WRN_k[\ell]$ (invocation of $WRN_k[\ell].\text{wrn}(j', v_i)$ at line 4) from which it obtains a value aux. If this value is not $\bot$, p_i returns it (line 5). If p_i executes all the iteration steps without deciding a value, it decides the value it proposed (line 7).

2.3.4 INFINITE HIERARCHY INSIDE THE "CONSENSUS NUMBER 1" LAND

The object family $\{WRN_k\}_{k \geq 3}$ defines an infinite hierarchy As already said, it has been shown in [22, 75, 128][7] that it is not possible for n processes, $n \geq k \geq 2$, to build $(k, k - 1)$-set agreement objects from atomic read/write registers. Moreover, as just seen, $(k, k - 1)$-set agreement objects and WRN_k objects are equivalent (from a computability point of view) in an n-process system where $n \geq k \geq 3$. It follows that WRN_k objects cannot either be built from atomic read/write registers.

On another side, given n processes communicating through atomic read/write registers and $(k, k - 1)$-set agreement objects where $k \geq 3$, it is not possible to solve consensus for two processes [38, 71, 84]. Hence, it follows that it is not possible to solve consensus for two processes from WRN_k objects when $n \geq k \geq 3$, and consequently their consensus number is 1.

Finally, considering an n-process system, where $n \geq k + x$ and $x \geq 1$, $(k + x, k - 1 + x)$-set agreement objects can be built from $(k, k - 1)$-set agreement objects and read/write registers, while $(k, k - 1)$-set agreement objects cannot be built from $(k + x, k - 1 + x)$-set agreement objects [38, 71]. It follows from the previous observations that, in an n-process system where $n \geq k \geq 3$, WRN_{k+1} objects can be built from WRN_k objects, while WRN_k objects cannot be built from WRN_{k+1} objects.

Let us remember that $\mathcal{CN}(2)$ denote any object whose consensus number is 2. The meaning of the symbol "<" was introduced in Section 2.2.2. Piecing together the previous observations we have:

$$\text{R/W Register} < \cdots < WRN_{k+1} < WRN_k < \cdots < WRN_3 < \mathcal{CN}(2).$$

The object WRN_2 Let p_0 and p_1 be two processes that access the object WRN_2. The value returned by process p_i, $i \in \{0, 1\}$ when it invokes $\text{wrn}(i, v_i)$ depends on the fact it is or not the first process to invoke it. According to the atomicity of WRN_2, if p_i is the first, its invocation $\text{wrn}(i, v_i)$ returns the value it proposes, namely v_i, otherwise it returns the value previously deposited in WRN_2, by the other process. Hence, WRN_2 allows two processes to solve consensus, i.e., $CN(WNR_2) = 2$. From a consensus number hierarchy's point of view, we consequently have $WRN_3 < WRN_2$.

---

[7]These articles were foundational in introducing topology to capture the behavior of distributed computations.

2.4   LIFE IN EACH "CONSENSUS NUMBER $\geq$ 2" LAND

For each value of $m \geq 2$, this section presents a countable infinite family of objects, denoted $AEG_{m,2}, AEG_{m,3}, ..., AEG_{m,k}$, etc., such that, for $k \geq 2$, we have

- the consensus number of $AEG_{m,k}$ is m,

- $AEG_{m,k}$ can be wait-free implemented from $AEG_{m,k+1}$, and

- $AEG_{m,k+1}$ cannot be wait-free implemented from $AEG_{m,k}$ objects and atomic read/write register in a system of $= mk + m + k$ processes.

It follows that, at each level $m \geq 2$ of the consensus hierarchy, there is an infinite countable family of objects that are totally ordered by their computability power. All the results presented in this section are due to Y. Afek, F. Ellen, and E. Gafni [3] (hence, the name "AEG" of these objects forged from the first letter of their surnames).

2.4.1   THE FAMILY OF $AEG_{m,k}$ OBJECTS

Let $m, k \geq 2$. The $AEG_{m,k}$ object seems partly inspired from the construction of k-set agreement objects in an n-process system from j-set agreement objects provided for free for any subset of m-processes. More precisely, an important result in this context is the following theorem due to [38, 71].[8]

Theorem 2.1   *Let $n > k$ and $m > j$ be positive integers. It is possible to wait-free build k-set agreement objects in a system of n processes from j-set agreement objects accessed by m processes if and only if:*

$$\left(k \geq j\right) \wedge \left(n\, j \leq m\, k\right) \wedge \left(k \geq \min\left(j\left\lceil \tfrac{n}{m}\right\rceil, j\left\lfloor \tfrac{n}{m}\right\rfloor + n - m\left\lfloor \tfrac{n}{m}\right\rfloor\right)\right).$$

The AEG object family is a generic family, with two genericity parameters $n, k \geq 2$. Each value of m gives rise to a sub-family $AEG_{m,k}$, in which each instance of the parameter $k \geq 2$ give rise to a specific object.

An $AEG_{m,k}$ object has a single atomic operation denoted aeg_write(), which is invoked at most once by each process. From a conceptual point of view, this object can be seen as an array with k entries, namely $A[1..k]$, plus a counter. A process invokes $\text{aeg\_write}_{m,k}(v)$, where v is the value it wants to write in the $AEG_{m,k}$ object. The first $(mk + k - 1)$ invocations of $\text{aeg\_write}_{m,k}(v)$ return a value that has been written in A, while all the following invocations return the default value $\perp$.

---

[8]This theorem was also instrumental in the design of an optimal k-set agreement algorithm in synchronous crash-prone message-passing systems [104], and in the establishment of a strong relation linking adaptive renaming and k-set agreement [56].

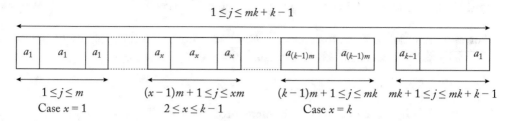

Figure 2.1: Value returned by the j-th invocation of $\mathsf{aeg\_write}_{m,k}()$.

More precisely, we have the following. Let us partition the sequence of the first $(mk + k - 1)$ invocations of $\mathsf{aeg\_write}_{m,k}()$ into k sub-sequences of m invocations each, and a last sub-sequence of $(k - 1)$ invocations (see Figure 2.1). Given the j-th invocation of $\mathsf{aeg\_write}_{m,k}()$, let CNT be an number of invocations $\mathsf{aeg\_write}_{m,k}()$ previously executed (hence, $CNT = j - 1$).

- Considering the first sub-sequence of m invocations of $\mathsf{aeg\_write}()$, let a_1 be the input parameter of its first invocation. This value is written in $A[1]$. The other $(m - 1)$ invocations do not write. Moreover, all these m invocations of this first sub-sequence return a_1 (Figure 2.1).

- The same occurs for each sub-sequence of m invocations of $\mathsf{aeg\_write}()$. For the x-th sub-sequence, $2 \le x \le k$, let a_x be the input parameter of its first invocation. This value is written in $A[x]$. The remaining $(m - 1)$ invocations of this sub-sequence do not write, and all the m invocations of this x-th sub-sequence return a_x.

- Finally, For $mk + 1 \le j \le mk + k - 1$, the j-th invocation of $\mathsf{aeg\_write}()$ does not write and returns the value in $A[mk + k - 1 - CNT]$, where CNT is the number of invocations of $\mathsf{aeg\_write}()$ previously executed.

Algorithm 2.6 is a simple translation of the previous description of $\mathsf{aeg\_write}_{m,k}()$. Let us remember that this operation is atomic. It is easy to see that an $\mathrm{AEG}_{m,k}$ object is deterministic.

2.4.2   THE CONSENSUS NUMBER OF AN $\mathrm{AEG}_{m,k}$ OBJECT IS m

Assuming $m \ge 2$, let us consider the operation described in Algorithm 2.7, which uses an underlying $\mathrm{AEG}_{m,k}$ object denoted $AEG_{m,k}$. It is easy to see that this algorithm solves consensus in an m-process system, and consequently the consensus number of $\mathrm{AEG}_{m,k}$ is at least m.

In a very interesting way, replacing in Algorithm 2.7 the set of m processes by a larger set of $n = mk + k - 1$ processes, we obtain the more general theorem.

Theorem 2.2   *Let $n = mk + k - 1$ and $m, k \ge 2$. A k-set agreement object can be implemented from an $\mathrm{AEG}_{m,k}$ object in an n-process system.*

Algorithm 2.6 The operation aeg_write$_{m,k}(v_i)$ invoked by p_i

```
operation aeg_write_m,k(v_i) is        % code for p_i
(1)     if (CNT = mk + k − 1) then return(⊥) end if;
(2)     if (CNT < mk)
(3)        then x_i ← ⌊CNT/m⌋ + 1;
(4)            if CNT = (x_i − 1)m then A[x_i] ← v end if
(5)        else  x_i ← km + k − (CNT + 1)
(6)     end if;
(7)     CNT ← CNT + 1;
(8)     return(A[x_i])
end of operation.
```

Algorithm 2.7 m-process consensus on top of an $\mathrm{AEG}_{m,k}$ object

```
operation propose_m,k(v_i) is  % code for p_i
(1)  r_i ← AEG_m,k.aeg_write(v_i);
(2)  return(r_i)
end of operation.
```

While it is simple to show that the consensus number of the $\mathrm{AEG}_{m,k}$ object is at least m, to show that it is exactly m is much more difficult, see [3] where is proved the following theorem.

Theorem 2.3   *Let $m, k \geq 2$. There is no deterministic algorithm implementing binary consensus from $\mathrm{AEG}_{m,k}$ objects and read/write registers in an $(m + 1)$-process system.*

It follows from Algorithm 2.7 and Theorem 2.3 that the consensus number of $\mathrm{AEG}_{m,k}$ is m.

Theorem 2.4   *Let $n \geq mk + k − 1$ and $m, k \geq 2$. An $\mathrm{AEG}_{m,k}$ object cannot be implemented from m-consensus objects and read/write registers in an n-process system.*

This theorem can be easily proved by contradiction. Consider $n = mk + k − 1$; let us assume the contrary, namely, an $\mathrm{AEG}_{m,k}$ object can be built from m-consensus objects in an n-process system. Using this $\mathrm{AEG}_{m,k}$ object, It follows from Theorem 2.2 that a k-set agreement object can be built in an $(km + k − 1)$-process system enriched with m-consensus objects. But, $\frac{mk+k−1}{k} = m + 1 − \frac{1}{k} > \frac{1}{m}$, which contradicts Theorem 2.1.

2.4.3   AN INFINITE HIERARCHY INSIDE EACH "CONSENSUS NUMBER m" LAND, $m \geq 2$

$\mathrm{AEG}_{m,k}$ can be implemented from $\mathrm{AEG}_{m,k+1}$ Algorithm 2.8 presents a simple construction of an $\mathrm{AEG}_{m,k}$ object from an $\mathrm{AEG}_{m,k+1}$, from which it follows that (while they have the same consensus number, namely m) $\mathrm{AEG}_{m,k+1}$ objects are at least as powerful as $\mathrm{AEG}_{m,k}$ objects.

This implementation is based on a specific initialization of the internal read/write registers implementing the underlying $AEG_{m,k+1}$ object. It is assumed that the value proposed by a process is a positive integer.

Algorithm 2.8 $AEG_{m,k}$ object from $AEG_{m,k+1}$ object

---

internal ad hoc initialization of the underlying $AEG_{m,k+1}$ object:
$CNT \leftarrow m; A[1] \leftarrow 0$.

operation aeg_write$_{m,k}(v)$ **is**   % code for any p_i
(1) $aux_i \leftarrow AEG_{m,k+1}$.aeg_write$_{m,k+1}(v + 1)$;
(2)   **if** $(aux_i > 0)$ **then** $r_i \leftarrow aux_i - 1$ **else** $r_i \leftarrow \bot$ **end if**;
(3)   return(r_i)
end of operation.

This algorithm consists in a simple "elimination" of the first entry of the underlying array $A[1..k + 1]$ implementing the $AEG_{m,k+1}$ object.

$AEG_{m,k+1}$ with respect to $AEG_{m,k}$ The following theorem is proved in [3], which states that an $AEG_{m,k+1}$ object is stronger than an $AEG_{m,k}$ object.

Theorem 2.5   *Let $m, k \geq 2$. An $AEG_{m,k+1}$ object cannot be implemented from $AEG_{m,k}$ objects and read/write registers in an $(mk + m + k)$-process system.*

An infinite hierarchy inside each "consensus number m" land, $m \geq 2$ It follows from the previous discussion that, at each level $m \geq 2$ of the consensus hierarchy, we have

$$CN(m - 1) < AEG_{m,2} \cdots < AEG_{m,k} < \cdots < AEG_{m,k+1} < \cdots < CN(m + 1).$$

2.5   CONCLUSION

The chapter was a short visit to the notion of consensus number, which is a central notion as soon as one is interested in universal wait-free constructions of objects defined by a sequential specification. The reader interested in more developments can consult [119] for asynchronous crash-prone shared memory systems, and [121] for asynchronous crash-prone message-passing systems.

The following intriguing issue remains open: "is 1 a special number?" More precisely, the family of objects WRN_k was introduced to show there is life in the land of consensus number 1, while the family of objects $AEG_{m,k}$ was introduced to show there is life in each level $m \geq 2$ of the consensus hierarchy. The question is then "is there a single object family—instead of two—that show there is life at all the levels of the consensus hierarchy?"

It follows from the results exposed in this chapter that, neither the notion of consensus number nor the notion of set agreement power characterizes the exact *computability power* of all the deterministic (and non-deterministic [112]) objects. On a close topic, the reader interested in the evolution of synchronization in the past 50 years can consult [114]. The interested reader will also find in [137] a study on the computability power of anonymous registers. Among other results, it is shown in [137] that, while the consensus number of an anonymous read/write bit is 1, this object is computationally weaker than a non-anonymous bit and weaker than an anonymous read/write register, whose consensus numbers are also 1.

CHAPTER 3

Distributed Recursivity

Recursion is a fundamental concept of sequential computing that allows for the design of simple and elegant algorithms. This chapter is a short introduction to recursive algorithms that compute distributed tasks (which generalize the notion of a function) in asynchronous distributed systems where communication is through atomic read/write registers, and any number of processes can crash. In such a context and differently from sequential and parallel recursion, the conceptual novelty lies in the fact that the aim of the recursion parameter is to allow each participating process to learn the number of processes that it sees as participating to the task computation.

Keywords: Asynchrony, Atomic read/write register, Branching time, Concurrency, Distributed algorithm, Concurrent object, Linear time, Participating process, Process crash failure, Recursion, Renaming, Shared memory, Task, Write-snapshot.

3.1   INTRODUCTION

Recursion   Recursion is a powerful algorithmic technique that consists in solving a problem of some size (where the size of the problem is measured by the number of its input data) by reducing it to problems of smaller size, and proceeding the same way until we arrive at basic problems that can be solved directly. This algorithmic strategy is often capture by the Latin terms "*divide ut imperes*."

Recursive algorithms are often simple and elegant. Moreover, they favor invariant-based reasoning, and their time complexity can be naturally captured by recurrence equations. In a few words, recursion is a fundamental concept addressed in all textbooks devoted to sequential programming (e.g., [41, 65, 77, 100] to cite a few). It is also important to say that, among the strong associations linking data structures and control structures, recursion is particularly well suited to trees and more generally to graph traversal [41].

Recursive algorithms are also used since a long time in parallel programming (e.g., [5]). In this case, parallel recursive algorithms are mainly extensions of sequential recursive algorithms, which exploit data independence. Simple examples of such algorithms are the parallel versions of the quicksort and mergesort sequential algorithms.

Recursion and distributed computing   In the domain of distributed computing, the first (to our knowledge) recursive algorithm that has been proposed is the algorithm solving the Byzantine general problem [96]. This algorithm is a message-passing synchronous algorithm. Its formulation is relatively simple and elegant, but it took many years to understand its deep nature (e.g., see [16] and textbooks such as [15, 99, 120]). Recursion has also been used to structure distributed systems to favor their design and satisfy dependability requirements [115].

Similarly to parallelism, recursion has been used in distributed algorithms to exploit data independence or provide time-efficient implementations of data structures. As an example, the distributed implementation of a store-collect object described in [12] uses a recursive algorithm to obtain an efficient tree traversal, which provides an efficient adaptive distributed implementation. As a second example, a recursive synchronous distributed algorithm has been introduced in [14] to solve the lattice agreement problem. This algorithm, which recursively divides a problem of size n into two sub-problems of size $n/2$, is then used to solve the snapshot problem [1]. Let us notice that an early formal treatment of concurrent recursion can be found in [51].

Capture the essence of distributed computing   One of the main issues of distributed computing lies in mastering the uncertainty created by the multiplicity and the geographical dispersion of computing entities, their asynchrony and the possibility of failures. Actually, the execution of an algorithm A is an implicit input of A. More precisely, a distributed execution (and consequently its results) is impacted by the environment (mainly asynchrony and failures), and two executions of the very same algorithm with the same local inputs can provide different results.

At some abstract level and from a "fundamentalist" point of view, such a distributed context is captured by the notion of a task, namely, the definition of a distributed computing unit which capture the essence of distributed computing [75]. Tasks are the distributed counterpart of mathematical functions encountered in sequential computing (where some of them are computable while others are not).

At the task level, recursion is interesting and useful mainly for the following reasons: it simplifies algorithm design, makes their proofs easier, and facilitates their analyze (thanks to topology [57, 106]).

Recursive algorithms for computable tasks   This chapter is on the design of recursive algorithms that compute tasks [57]. It appears that, for each process participating to a task, the recursion parameter x is not related to the size of a data structure but to the number of processes that the invoking process perceives as participating to the task computation. In a very interesting way, it follows from this feature that it is possible to design a general pattern, which can be appropriately instantiated for particular tasks.

When designing such a pattern, the main technical difficulty come from the fact that processes may run concurrently, and, at any time, distinct processes can be executing at the same recursion level or at different recursion levels. To cope with such an issue, recursion relies on an underlying data structure (basically, an array of atomic read/write registers) which keeps the current state of each recursion level.

After having introduced the general recursion pattern, this chapter instantiates it to solve two tasks, namely, the write-snapshot task [23] and the renaming task [10]. Interestingly, the first instantiation of the pattern is based on a notion of linear time (there is single sequence of recursive calls, and each participating process executes a prefix of it), while the second instantiation is based on a notion of branching time (a process executes a prefix of a single branch of the recursion tree whose branches individually capture all possible execution paths).

In addition to its methodological dimension related to the new use of recursion in a distributed setting, this chapter has a pedagogical flavor in the sense that it focuses on, and explains, fundamental notions of distributed computing. Said differently, an aim of this chapter is to provide the reader with a better view of the nature of fault-tolerant distributed recursion when the processes are concurrent, asynchronous, communicate through read/write registers, and are prone to crash failures.

Content of the chapter   Section 3.2 presents the computation model and the notion of a task. Then, Section 3.3 introduces the basic recursive pattern in which the recursion parameter of a process represents its current approximation of the number of processes it sees as participating. The next two sections present instantiations of the pattern that solve the write-snapshot task (Section 3.4) and the renaming task (Section 3.5). (While this chapter adopts a programming methodology perspective, the interested reader will find in [106] a topological perspective of recursion in distributed computing.)

3.2   COMPUTATION MODEL, DISTRIBUTED TASK, AND EXAMPLES OF TASKS

3.2.1   COMPUTATION MODEL

Process model   The computing model is the classic $\mathcal{CARW}[\emptyset]$ model (defined in Chapter 1). The n processes are denoted $p_1, \ldots, p_n$. A process is a deterministic state machine. The integer i is called the index of p_i. The indexes can only be used for addressing purposes. Each process p_i has a name—or identity—id_i. Initially, a process p_i knows only id_i, n, and the fact that no two processes have the same initial name. Moreover, process names belong to a totally ordered set and this is known by the processes (hence, two identities can be compared).

The processes are asynchronous in the sense that the relative execution speed of different processes is arbitrary and can varies with time, and there is no bound on the time it takes for a process to execute a step.

Communication model and local memory   The processes communicate by accessing atomic read/write registers. Atomic means that, from an external observer point of view, each read or write operation appears as if it has been executed at a single point of the time line between its start and end events [76, 92].

Each atomic register is a single-writer/multi-reader (SWMR) register. This means that, given any register, a single process (statically determined) can write in this register, while all the processes can read it. Let $X[1..n]$ be an array of atomic registers whose entries are the process indexes. By convention, $X[i]$ can be written only by p_i. Atomic registers are denoted with uppercase letters. All shared registers are initialized to a default value denoted $\bot$ and no process can write $\bot$ in a register. Hence, the meaning of $\bot$ is to state that the corresponding register has not yet been written.

A process can have local variables. Those are denoted with lowercase letters and subscripted by the index of the corresponding process. As an example, aaa_i denotes the local variable aaa of process p_i.

Failure model   The atomic read/write registers are assumed to experience no failure. (For the interested reader, the construction of atomic reliable registers from basic atomic registers which can fail—crash, omission, or Byzantine failures—is addressed in [116].)

A process may crash (halt prematurely). A process executes correctly until it possibly crashes, and after it has crashed (if ever it does), it executes no step. Given a run, a process that crashes is *faulty*, otherwise it is *non-faulty*.

Any number of processes may crash (*wait-free* model [66]). Let us observe that the wait-free model prevents implicitly the use of locks (this is because a process that owns a lock and crashes before releasing it can block the whole system). (Locks can be implemented from atomic read/write registers only in reliable systems [116].)

3.2.2   THE NOTION OF A DISTRIBUTED TASK

Informal definition   As indicated in the Introduction, a *distributed task* is the distributed counterpart of a mathematical function encountered in sequential computing.

In a task each process p_i has a private input value in_i and, given a run, the n input values constitute the input vector I of the considered run. Each process knows initially only its input value, which is usually called *proposed value*. Then, from an operational point of view, the processes have to coordinate and communicate in such a way that each process p_i computes an output value out_i and the n output values define an output vector O, such that $O \in \Delta(I)$ where Δ is the mapping defining the task. An output value is also called *decided* value. The way a distributed task extends the notion of a sequential function is described in Figure 3.1, where the left side represents a classical a sequential function and the right side represents a distributed task.

As in sequential computing (Turing machines) where there are computable functions and uncomputable functions, there are computable tasks and uncomputable tasks. As we will see later, write-snapshot and renaming are computable in asynchronous read/write systems despite asynchrony and any number of process failures, while consensus is not [50, 66, 97].

Formal definition   A *distributed task* T is a triple $\langle \mathcal{I}, \mathcal{O}, \Delta \rangle$ where

- $\mathcal{I}$ is the set of allowed input vectors,

- $\mathcal{O}$ is the set of allowed output vectors, and

- Δ is a mapping of $\mathcal{I}$ into $\mathcal{O}$ such that $(\forall I \in \mathcal{I}) \Rightarrow (\Delta(I) \in \mathcal{O})$.

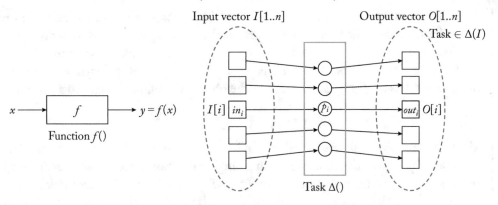

Figure 3.1: Function (left) and task (right).

Hence, $I[i]$ and $O[i]$ are the values proposed and decided by p_i, respectively, while $\Delta(I)$ defines the set of output vectors that can be decided from the input vector I. (More developments on the definition of tasks and their relation with topology can be found in [72, 75].)

If one or several processes p_i, ..., p_j do not participate or crash before deciding an output value, we have $O[i] = \ldots = O[j] = \bot$, and the vector O has then to be such that there is a vector $O' \in \Delta(I)$ that covers O, i.e., $(O[i] \neq \bot) \Rightarrow (O'[i] = O[i])$.

A simple example: the binary consensus task   In this task, a process proposes a value from the set $\{0, 1\}$, and all the non-faulty processes have to decide the same value which has to be a proposed value. Let X_0 and X_1 be the vector of size n containing only zeros and only ones, respectively.

The set $\mathcal{I}$ of input vectors is the set of all the vectors of zeros and ones. The set $\mathcal{O}$ of output vectors is $\{X_0, X_1\}$. The mapping Δ is such that (i) $\Delta($ any vector except $X_0, X_1) = \mathcal{O}$, (ii) $\Delta(X_0) = X_0$, and (iii) $\Delta(X_1) = X_1$.

Solving a task   In the context of this chapter, a distributed algorithm $\mathcal{A}$ is a set of n local automata (one per process) that communicate through atomic read/write registers.

The algorithm $\mathcal{A}$ solve a task T if, in any run in which each process proposes a value such that the input vector belongs to $\mathcal{I}$, each non-faulty process decides a value, and the vector O of output values belongs to the set $\Delta(I)$.

Tasks vs. objects   A task is a mathematical object. From a programming point of view, a concurrent object can be associated with a task (a concurrent object is an object that can be accessed by several processes). Such an object is a one-shot object that provides the processes with a single operation ("one-shot" means that a process can invoke the object operation at most once). More developments on the relation between tasks and objects can be found in [32].

To adopt a more intuitive presentation, the two tasks that are presented below use their object formulation. This formulation expresses the mapping Δ defining a task by a set of properties that the operation invocations have to satisfy. These properties can be more restrictive than Δ. This comes from the fact that there is no notion of time/concurrency/communication pattern in Δ, while the set of properties defining the object can implicitly refer to such notions.

3.2.3   THE WRITE-SNAPSHOT TASK

The write-snapshot task was introduced in [23] (where it is called *immediate snapshot*). A write-snapshot object provides processes with a single operation denoted write_snapshot(). When a process p_i invokes this operation, it supplies as input parameters its identity id_i and the value it wants to deposit into the write-snapshot object. Its invocation returns a set $view_i$ composed of pairs (id_j, v_j).

As previously indicated, the specification Δ is expressed here a set of properties that the invocations of write_snapshot() have to satisfy.

- Self-inclusion. $\forall\, i : (id_i, v_i) \in view_i$.

- Containment. $\forall\, i, j : (view_i \subseteq view_j) \vee (view_j \subseteq view_i)$.

- Simultaneity. $\forall\, i, j : [((id_j, v_j) \in view_i) \wedge ((id_i, v_i) \in view_j)] \Rightarrow (view_i = view_j)$.

- Termination. Any invocation of write_snapshot() by a non-faulty process terminates.

A write-snapshot combines in a single operation the write of a value (here a pair (id_i, v_i)) and a snapshot [1] of the set of pairs already or concurrently written. Self-inclusion states that a process sees its write. Containment states the views of the pairs deposited are ordered by containment. Simultaneity states that if each of the two processes sees the pair deposited by the other one, they have the same view of the deposited pairs. Finally, the termination property states that the progress condition associated with operation invocations is wait-freedom, which means that an invocation by a non-faulty process terminates whatever the behavior of the other processes (which can be slow, crashed, or not participating). An iterative implementation of write-snapshot can be found in [23, 116].

3.2.4   THE ADAPTIVE RENAMING TASK

This task has been introduced in [10] in the context of asynchronous crash-prone message-passing systems. Thereafter, a lot of renaming algorithms suited to read/write communication have been proposed. An introduction to shared memory renaming, and associated lower bounds, is presented in [31].

While there are only n process identities, the space name is usually much bigger than n (as a simple example this occurs when the name of a machine is the IP address). The aim of the adaptive renaming task is to allow the processes to obtain new names from a new name space which has to depend only on the number p of processes that want to obtain a new name $(1 \le p \le n)$, and be as small as possible. It is shown in [75] that $2p - 1$ is a lower bound on the size of the new name space.

When considering the adaptive renaming task from the point of view of its associated one-shot object, a process p_i that wants to acquire a new name invokes an operation denoted new_name(id_i). The set of invocations has to satisfy the following set of properties.

- Validity. The size of the new name space is $2p - 1$.

- Agreement. No two processes obtain the same new name.

- Termination. Any invocation of new_name() by a non-faulty process terminates.

As for the write-snapshot task, the termination property states that a non-faulty process that invokes the operation new_name() obtains a new name whatever the behavior of the other processes. Agreement states the consistency condition associated with new names. Validity states the domain of the new names: if a single process wants to obtain a new name, it obtains the name 1, if only two processes invoke new_name() they obtain new names in the set $\{1, 2, 3\}$, etc. This shows that the termination property (wait-freedom progress condition) has a cost in the size of the new name space: while only p new names are needed, the new name space needs $(p - 1)$ additional potential new names to allow the invocations issued by non-faulty processes to always terminate.

3.3   A PATTERN FOR RECURSIVE DISTRIBUTED ALGORITHMS

The recursion parameter   As already announced, the recursion parameter (denoted x) in the algorithms solving the tasks we are interested is the number of processes that the invoking process perceives as participating processes. As initially a process has no knowledge of how many processes are participating, it conservatively considers that all other processes participate, and consequently issues a main call with $x = n$.

Atomic read/write registers and local variables   The pattern manages an array $SM[n..1]$, where each $SM[x]$ is a sub-array of size n such that $SM[x][i]$ can be written only by p_i. A process p_i starts executing the recursion level x by depositing a value in $SM[x][i]$. From then on, it is a participating process at level x.

Each process manages locally three variables whose scope is a recursive invocation. $sm_i[n..1]$ is used to save a copy of the current value of $SM[x][1..n]$; $part_i$ keeps the number of processes that p_i sees as participating at level x; and res_i is used to save the result returned by the current invocation.

The recursion pattern   Algorithm 3.1 describes the generic recursive pattern. The invoking process p_i first deposits its input parameter value in $SM[x][i]$ (line 1), and read the content of

---

Algorithm 3.1 Concurrency-related distributed recursive pattern

---

```
operation recursive_pattern(x, input) is                      % code for process pᵢ
(1)      SM[x][i] ← input;
(2)      for each j ∈ {1, ..., n} do smᵢ[j] ← SM[x][j] end for;
(3)      partᵢ ← |{smᵢ[j] ≠ ⊥}|;
(4)      if (partᵢ = x) then statements specific to the task, possibly including a recursive call;
(5)                          computation of resᵢ
(6)                  else  resᵢ ← recursive_pattern(x − 1, input)
(7)      end if;
(8)      return(resᵢ)
end of operation.
```

---

the shared memory attached to its recursion level x (line 2). Let us notice that the entries of the array $SM[x][1..n]$ are read in any order and asynchronously. Then, p_i computes the number of processes it sees as participating in the recursion level x (line 3), and checks if this number is equal to its current recursion level x.

- if $x = part_i$ (lines 4–5), p_i discovers that x processes are involved in the recursion level x. In this case, it executes statements at the end of which it computes a local result res_i. These local statements are task-dependent and may or not involve a recursive call with recursion level $x − 1$.

- if $x \neq part_i$, p_i sees less than x processes participating to the recursion level x. In this case, it invokes the recursion pattern at level $x − 1$ with the same input parameter *input*, and continues until it attains a recursion level $x' \leq x − 1$ at which it sees exactly x' processes that have attained this recursion level x'.

A process p_i starts with its recursion parameter x equal n, and then its recursion parameter decreases until the invoking process returns a result. Hence, a process executes at most n recursive calls before terminating. The correctness proof of this recursive pattern is the same as the one of Theorem 3.1 which considers its write-snapshot instantiation.

Linear time vs. branching time   If line 4 does not include a recursive call, the recursive pattern is a linear time pattern. Each participating process executes line 6 until its stops at line 4 (or crashes before). Hence, each process executes a prefix of the same sequence of recursive calls, each with its initial input parameter *input*. The algorithm, whose instantiation from the recursive pattern is described in Section 3.4, is a linear time implementation of write-snapshot.

If there are recursive calls at line 4, the recursive pattern is a branching time pattern. Such a recursion pattern is characterized by a tree of recursive calls, and a participating process executes a prefix of a single branch of this tree. In this case, each $SM[x]$ is composed of several sub-arrays, each of them being an array of n SWMR atomic registers. The algorithm, whose instantiation from the recursive pattern is described in Section 3.5, is a branching time implementation of renaming.

3.4   LINEAR TIME RECURSION

3.4.1   A RECURSIVE WRITE-SNAPSHOT ALGORITHM

Algorithm 3.2 (introduced in [57]) is an instantiation of the recursive pattern that implements the write-snapshot operation. The representation adopted here is from [116]. This instantiation is nearly the same as the original recursive pattern. The input parameter *input* of a process p_i is now the pair $\langle id_i, v_i \rangle$.

The line numbering is the same as in the recursive pattern. As there is no specific statement to instantiate at line 4 of the recursive pattern, its lines 4 and 5 are instantiated by a single line denoted $4 + 5$.

A process p_i invokes first write_snapshot$(n, \langle id_i, v_i \rangle)$ where v_i is the value it wants to deposit in the write-snapshot object.

Algorithm 3.2 A recursive write-snapshot distributed algorithm

---

        operation write_snapshot$(x, \langle id_i, v_i \rangle)$ **is**   % code for process p_i
(1) $SM[x][i] \leftarrow \langle id_i, v_i \rangle$;
(2)   **for each** $j \in \{1, \dots, n\}$ **do** $sm_i[j] \leftarrow SM[x][j]$ **end for**;
(3) $part_i \leftarrow |\{sm_i[j] \neq \bot\}|$;
(4+5) **if** $(part_i = x)$ **then** $res_i \leftarrow \{sm_i[j] \neq \bot\}$
              else $res_i \leftarrow$ write_snapshot$(x - 1, \langle id_i, v_i \rangle)$
(7)   **end if**;
(8)   return(res_i)
    end of operation.

As already said, the recursion of this algorithm is a linear time recursion. This appears clearly from the arrays of atomic read/write registers accessed by the recursive calls issued by the processes: each process accesses first $SM[n]$, then $SM[n-1]$, etc., until it stops at $SM[x]$ where $n \geq x \geq 1$.

3.4.2   PROOF OF THE ALGORITHM

Theorem 3.1   *Algorithm 3.2 implements a write-snapshot object. For a process p_i, the step complexity (number of shared memory accesses) for a process p_i is $O(n(n - |res_i| + 1))$, where res_i is the set returned by the invocation of* write_snapshot() *issued by p_i.*

Proof   This proof is from [57, 116]. While a process terminates an invocation when it executes the return() statement at line 7, we say that it terminates at lines 4 or 5, according to the line where the returned value res_i has been computed.

Claim C. If at most x processes invoke write_snapshot($x, -$), (a) at most $(x - 1)$ processes invoke write_snapshot($x - 1, -$), and (b) at least one process stops at line 4 of its invocation of write_snapshot($x, -$).

Proof of claim C. Assuming that at most x processes invoke write_snapshot($x, -$), let p_k be the last process that writes into $SM[x][1..n]$ (as the registers are atomic, the notion of "last" is well-defined). We necessarily have $part_k \leq x$. If p_k finds $part_k = x$, it stops at line 4. Otherwise, we have $part_k < x$ and p_k invokes write_snapshot($x - 1, -$) at line 5. But in this case, as p_k is the last process that wrote into the array $SM[x][1..n]$, it follows from $part_k < x$ that fewer than x processes have written into $SM[x][1..n]$, and consequently, at most $(x - 1)$ processes invoke write_snapshot($x - 1, -$). End of the proof of claim C.

To prove termination, let us consider a non-faulty process p_i that invokes write_snapshot($n, -$). It follows from Claim C and the fact that at most n processes invoke write_snapshot($n, -$) that either p_i stops at that invocation or belongs to the set of at most $(n - 1)$ processes that invoke write_snapshot($n - 1, -$). It then follows, by induction from the claim C, that if p_i has not stopped during a previous invocation, it is the only process that invokes write_snapshot($1, -$). It then follows from the text of the algorithm that it stops at that invocation.

The proof of the self-inclusion property is trivial. Before stopping at recursion level x (line 4), a process p_i has written v_i into $SM[x][i]$ (line 1), and consequently we have then $(id_i, v_i) \in view_i$, which concludes the proof of the self-inclusion property.

To prove the self-containment and simultaneity properties, let us first consider the case of two processes that return at the same recursion level x. If a process p_i returns at line 4 of recursion level x, let $res_i[x]$ denote the corresponding value of res_i. Among the processes that stop at recursion level x, let p_i be the last process which writes into $SM[x][1..n]$. As p_i stops, this means that $SM[x][1..n]$ has exactly x entries different from $\perp$ and (due to Claim C) no more of its entries will be set to a non-$\perp$ value. It follows that, as any other process p_j that stops at recursion level x reads x non-$\perp$ entries from $SM[x][1..n]$, we have $res_i[x] = res_j[x]$ which proves the properties.

Let us now consider the case of two processes p_i and p_j that return at line 5 of recursion level x and y, respectively, with $x > y$ (i.e., p_i returns $res_i[x]$ while p_j returns $res_j[y]$). The self-containment follows then from $x > y$ and the fact that p_j has written into all the arrays $SM[z][1..n]$ with $n \geq z \geq y$, from which we conclude that $res_j[y] \subseteq res_i[x]$. Moreover, as $x > y$, p_i has not written into $SM[y][1..n]$ while p_j has written into $SM[x][1..n]$, and consequently $(id_j, v_j) \in res_i[x]$ while $(id_i, v_i) \notin res_j[y]$, from which both the containment and immediacy properties follow.

As far as the number of shared memory accesses is concerned we have the following. Let res be the set returned by an invocation of write_snapshot($n, -$). Each recursive invocation costs $n + 1$ shared memory accesses (lines 1 and 2). Moreover, the sequence of invocations, namely write_snapshot($n, -$), write_snapshot($n - 1, -$), etc., until write_snapshot($|res|, -$)

Table 3.1: Write-snapshot execution: an example

	p_1	p_2	p_3	p_4	p_5
τ_1			ws(5, $\langle id_3, v_3 \rangle$)		
τ_2			ws(4, $\langle id_3, v_3 \rangle$)		
τ_3			crashes		
τ_4				ws(5, $\langle id_4, v_4 \rangle$)	
τ_5				... ws(1, $\langle id_4, v_4 \rangle$)	
τ_6				$\{\langle id_4, v_4 \rangle\}$	
τ_7	ws(5, $\langle id_1, v_1 \rangle$)	ws(5, $\langle id_2, v_2 \rangle$)			
τ_8	ws(4, $\langle id_1, v_1 \rangle$)	ws(4, $\langle id_2, v_2 \rangle$)			
τ_9	res_1	res_2			

Table 3.2: Write-snapshot execution: continuing the example

	p_1	p_2	p_3	p_4	p_5
τ_{10}			ws(3, $\langle id_3, v_3 \rangle$)		
τ_{11}			ws(2, $\langle id_3, v_3 \rangle$)		
τ_{12}			res_3		

(where $x = |res|$ is the recursion level at which the recursion stops) contains $n - |res| + 1$ invocations. It follows that the step complexity for a process p_i is $O(n(n - |res_i| + 1))$ accesses to atomic registers. □ *Theorem* 3.1

3.4.3   EXAMPLE OF AN EXECUTION

This section described simple executions where $n = 5$ and process p_5 crashes before taking any step (or—equivalently—does not participate). These executions are described in Tables 3.1 and 3.2. In these tables write_snapshot() is abbreviated as ws().

A first execution

1. At time τ_1, process p_3 invokes write_snapshot(5, $\langle id_3, v_3 \rangle$). This triggers at time τ_2 the recursive invocation write_snapshot(4, $\langle id_3, v_3 \rangle$). Then, p_3 crashes after it has written id_3 into $SM[4][3]$ at time τ_3.

2. At a later time τ_4, process p_4 invokes write_snapshot(5, $\langle id_4, v_4 \rangle$), which recursively ends up with the invocation write_snapshot(1, $\langle id_4, v_4 \rangle$) at time τ_5, and consequently p_4 returns the singleton set $\{\langle id_4, v_4 \rangle\}$ at time τ_6.

3. At time τ_7, both the process p_1 and the process p_2 start executing synchronously: namely, p_1 invokes write_snapshot(5, $\langle id_1, v_1 \rangle$), while p_2 invokes write_snapshot(5, $\langle id_2, v_2 \rangle$), which entails

4. At time τ_8—always synchronously—the recursive invocation of write_snapshot(4, $\langle id_1, v_1 \rangle$) by p_1 and the recursive invocation of write_snapshot(4, $\rangle id_2, v_2 \rangle$) by p_2. As $SM[4]$ contains four non-$\perp$ entries, both the processes p_1 and p_2 return res_1 and res_2 which are such that $res_1 = res_2 = \{\langle id_1, v_1 \rangle, \langle id_2, v_2 \rangle, \langle id_3, v_3 \rangle, \langle id_3, v_4 \rangle\}$.

Continuing the example Let us assume that instead of crashing at time τ_3, p_3 paused for an arbitrary long period starting after it has read $SM[4][1..5]$ (hence, it has seen only two non-$\perp$ values in $SM[4]$).

1. At time τ_{10}, p_3 wakes up and, as $part_3 \neq 4$, it recursively invokes write_snapshot(3, (id_3, v_3)), which entails at time τ_{11} the invocation write_snapshot(2, (id_3, v_3)).

2. As at time τ_{12}, the shared array $SM[2]$ contains two non-$\perp$ values, process p_4 returns $res_3 = \{(id_3, v_3), (id_3, v_4)\}$.

The reader can check that, if before pausing at time τ_3, p_3 has read only $SM[4][4]$ and $SM[4][5]$, it will read the other entries $SM[4][1]$, $SM[4][2]$, and $SM[4][3]$, when it wakes up, and its invocation write_snapshot(4, (id_3, v_3)) will stop the recursion and return $res_3 = res_1 = res_2$.

3.5   BRANCHING TIME RECURSION

3.5.1   A RECURSIVE RENAMING ALGORITHM

An instance of the recursive pattern implementing adaptive renaming is described in Figure 3.3. This recursive implementation, inspired from the sketch of an algorithm skeleton succinctly described in [57], is described in [113], where it is proved correct. As for the previous recursive algorithm, the representation adopted here is from [57, 116]. The core of this recursive algorithm is the instantiation of line 4 of the recursive pattern, where branching time recursion appears.

Underlying idea: the case of two processes The base case is when $n = 2$. A process p_i first writes its identity id_i in the shared memory, and then reads the content of the memory.

- If, according to what it has read from the shared memory, a process sees only itself, it adopts the new name 1.

- Otherwise, it knows its identity and the one of the other process (id_j). It then compares its identity id_i and id_j, and does the following: if $id_i > id_j$, it adopts the new name 3, if $id_i < id_j$, it adopts the new name 2.

The new name space is consequently $[1..2p - 1]$, where p (number of participating processes) is 1 or 2.

The underlying shared memory The shared memory $SM[n..1]$ accessed by processes is now a three-dimensional array $SM[n..1, 1..2n - 1, \{\text{up}, \text{down}\}]$ such that $SM[x, \text{first}, \text{dir}]$ is an array of n atomic read/write registers. $SM[x, \text{first}, \text{dir}][i]$ can be written only by p_i but can be read by all processes.

From a notational point of view, $\text{up} = 1 = \overline{\text{down}}$ and $\text{down} = -1 = \overline{\text{up}}$.

When more than two processes participate Algorithm 3.3 implements recursive renaming. A process invokes first $\text{new\_name}(n, 1, \text{up}, id_i)$. It then recursively invokes $\text{new\_name}(x, 1, \text{up}, id_i)$, until the recursion level x is equal to the number of processes that p_i sees as competing for a new name.

As we are about to see, given a pair $(\text{first}, \text{dir})$, the algorithm ensures that at most x processes invoke $\text{new\_name}(x, \text{first}, \text{dir}, -)$. These processes compete for new names in a space name of size $2x - 1$ which is the interval $[\text{first}..\text{first} + (2x - 2)]$ if $\text{dir} = \text{up}$, and $[\text{first} - (2x - 2)..\text{first}]$ if $\text{dir} = \text{down}$. Hence, the value up is used to indicate that the concerned processes are renaming "from left to right" (as far as the new names are concerned), while down is used to indicate that the concerned processes are renaming "from right to left" (this is developed below when explaining the splitter behavior of the underlying read/write registers). Hence, a process p_i considers initially the renaming space $[1..2n - 1]$, and then (as far p_i is concerned) this space will shrink at each recursive invocation (going up or going down) until p_i obtains a new name.

Algorithm 3.3 A recursive adaptive renaming algorithm

```
        operation new_name(x, first, dir, id_i) is
(1)           SM[x, first, dir][i] ← id_i;
(2)           for each j ∈ {1, ..., n} do sm_i[j] ← SM[x, first, dir][j] end for;
(3)           part_i ← |{sm_i[j] ≠ ⊥}|;
(4+5).1       if (part_i = x) then last ← first = dir(2x − 2);
(4+5).2                            if (id_i = max(sm_i))
(4+5).3                                then res_i ← last
(4+5).4                                else res_i ← new_name(x − 1, last + dir, dir, id_i))
(4+5).5                            end if
(6)                          else res_i ← new_name(x − 1, first, dir, id_i))
(7)           end if;
(8)           return(res_i)
        end operation.
```

The recursive algorithm   Lines 1–3 and 6–8 are the same as in the recursive pattern where $SM[x]$ is replaced by $SM[x, first, dir]$. The lines which are specific to adaptive renaming are the statements in the **then** part of the recursive pattern (lines 4–5). These statements are instantiated by the new lines $(4 + 5).1$–$(4 + 5).5$, which constitute an appropriate instantiation suited adaptive renaming.

For each triple (x, f, d), all invocations new_name$(-, x, f, d)$ coordinate their respective behavior with the help of the size n array of atomic read/write registers $SM[x, f, d][1..n]$. At line $(4 + 5).2$, max(sm_i) denotes the greatest process identity present in sm_i. As a process p_i deposits its identity in $SM[x, first, dir][i]$ before reading $SM[x, first, dir][1..n]$, it follows that sm_i contains at least one process identity when read by p_i.

Let us observe that, if only p processes invoke new_name$(n, 1, up, -)$, $p < n$, then all of them will invoke the algorithm recursively, first with new_name$(n - 1, 1, up)$, then new_name$(n - 2, 1, up)$, etc., until new_name$(p, 1, up, -)$. Only at this point, the behavior of a participating process p_i depend on the concurrency pattern (namely, it may or may not invoke the algorithm recursively, and with either up or down).

Splitter behavior associated with $SM[x, first, dir]$ (The notion of a splitter has been informally introduced in [93].) Considering the (at most) x processes that invoke new_name$(x, first, dir, -)$, the splitter behavior associated with the array of atomic registers $SM[x, first, dir]$ is defined by the following properties. Let $x' = x - 1$.

- At most, $x' = x - 1$ processes invoke new_name$(x - 1, first, dir, -)$ (line 6). Hence, these processes will obtain new names in an interval of size $(2x' - 1)$ as follows:

  - if $dir =$ up, the new names will be in the "going up" interval $[first..first + (2x' - 2)]$ or

  - if $dir =$ down, the new names will be in the "going down" interval $[first - (2x' - 2)..first]$.

- At most, $x' = x - 1$ processes invoke new_name$(x - 1, last + \overline{dir}, \overline{dir})$ (line $(4 + 5).4$), where $last = first + dir(2x - 2)$ (line $(4 + 5).1$). Hence, these $x' = x - 1$ processes will obtain their new names in a renaming space of size $(2x' - 1)$ starting at $last + 1$ and going from left to right if $\overline{dir} =$ up, or starting at $last - 1$ and going from right to left if $\overline{dir} =$ down. Let us observe that the value $last \pm 1$ is considered as the starting name because the slot $last$ is reserved for the new name of the process (if any) that stops during its invocation of new_name$(x, first, dir)$ (see next item).

- At most, one process "stops," i.e., defines its new name as $last = first + dir(2x - 2)$ (lines $(4 + 5).2$ and $(4 + 5).3$). Let us observe that the only process p_k that can stop is the one such that id_k has the greatest value in the array $SM[x, first, dir][1..n]$ which then contains exactly x identities.

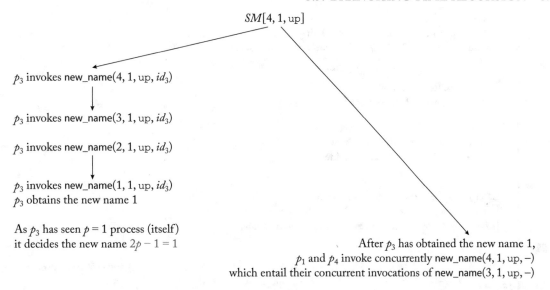

Figure 3.2: Recursive renaming: first, p_3 executes alone.

3.5.2   EXAMPLE OF AN EXECUTION

A proof of the previous algorithm can be found in [116]. This section presents an example of an execution of this algorithm. It considers four processes: p_1, p_2, p_3, and p_4.

First: process p_3 executes alone   Process p_3 invokes new_name$(4, 1, \text{up}, id_1)$ while (for the moment) no other process invokes the renaming operation. It follows from the algorithm that p_3 invokes recursively new_name$(3, 1, \text{up}, id_1)$, then new_name$(2, 1, \text{up}, id_1)$, and finally new_name$(1, 1, \text{up}, id_1)$. During the last invocation, it obtains the new name 1. This is illustrated in Figure 3.2. As, during its execution, p_3 sees only $p = 1$ process (namely, itself), it decides consistently in the new name space $[1..2p - 1] = 1$.

Then: processes p_1 and p_4 invoke new_name()   After p_3 has obtained a new name, both p_1 and p_4 invoke new_name$(4, 1, \text{up}, -)$ (see Figure 3.3). As they see only three processes that have written their identities into $SM[4, 1, \text{up}]$, both concurrently invoke new_name$(3, 1, \text{up}, -)$ and consequently both compute $last = 1 + (2 * 3 - 2) = 5$. Hence, their new name space is $[1..5]$.

Now, let us assume that p_1 stops executing while p_4 executes alone. Moreover, let $id_1, id_4 < id_3$. As it has not the greatest identity among the processes that have accessed $SM[3, 1, \text{up}]$ (namely, the processes p_1, p_3, and p_4), p_4 invokes first new_name$(2, 4, \text{down}, id_4)$ and then recursively new_name$(1, 4, \text{down}, id_4)$, and finally obtains the new name 4.

After process p_4 has obtained its new name, process p_1 continues its execution and invokes new_name$(2, 4, \text{down}, id_1)$ and computes $last = 4 - (2 \times 2 - 2) = 2$. The behavior of

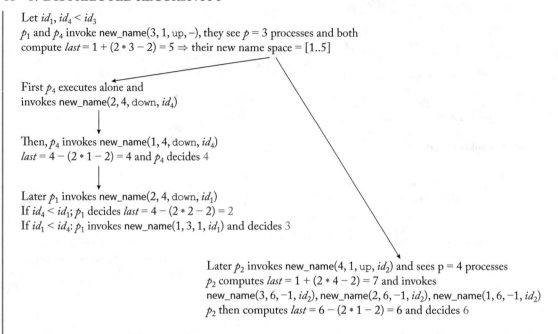

Let id_1, $id_4 < id_3$
p_1 and p_4 invoke new_name(3, 1, up, −), they see $p = 3$ processes and both
compute $last = 1 + (2 * 3 − 2) = 5 \Rightarrow$ their new name space = [1..5]

First p_4 executes alone and
invokes new_name(2, 4, down, id_4)

Then, p_4 invokes new_name(1, 4, down, id_4)
$last = 4 − (2 * 1 − 2) = 4$ and p_4 decides 4

Later p_1 invokes new_name(2, 4, down, id_1)
If $id_4 < id_1$; p_1 decides $last = 4 − (2 * 2 − 2) = 2$
If $id_1 < id_4$: p_1 invokes new_name(1, 3, 1, id_1) and decides 3

Later p_2 invokes new_name(4, 1, up, id_2) and sees p = 4 processes
p_2 computes $last = 1 + (2 * 4 − 2) = 7$ and invokes
new_name(3, 6, −1, id_2), new_name(2, 6, −1, id_2), new_name(1, 6, −1, id_2)
p_2 then computes $last = 6 − (2 * 1 − 2) = 6$ and decides 6

Figure 3.3: Recursive renaming: p_1 and p_4 invoke new_name(4, 1, up, −).

p_1 depends then on the values of id_1 and id_4. If $id_4 < id_1$, p_1 decides the name $last = 4 − (2 \times 2 − 2) = 2$. If $id_4 > id_1$, p_1 invokes new_name(1, 3, 1, id_1) and finally decides the name 3.

Finally, if later p_2 invokes new_name(4, 1, up, id_2), it sees that the splitter $SM[4, 1, \text{up}]$ was accessed by four processes. Hence, p_2 computes $last = 1 + (2 \times 4 − 2) = 1$, and consequently invokes recursively new_name(3, 6, down, id_1), new_name(2, 6, down, id_1), new_name(1, 6, down, id_1), at the end of which it computes $last = 6 + (2 \times 1 − 2) = 6$ and decides the name 6.

The multiplicity of branching times appears clearly on this example. As an example, the branch of time experienced by p_3 (which is represented by the sequence of accesses to $SM[4, 1, \text{up}]$, $SM[3, 1, \text{up}]$, $SM[2, 1, \text{up}]$, and $SM[1, 1, \text{up}]$) is different from the branch of time experienced by p_4 (which is represented by the sequence of accesses to $SM[4, 1, \text{up}]$, $SM[3, 1, \text{up}]$, $SM[2, 4, \text{down}]$, and $SM[1, 4, \text{up}]$).

Let us observe that the new name space attributed to the $p = 3$ processes p_1, p_3, and p_4 (the only ones that, upto now, have invoked new_name(4, 1, up)()) is $[1..2p − 1] = [1..5]$.

Finally: process p_2 invokes new_name() Let us now assume that p_2 invokes new_name(4, 1, up, id_2). Moreover, let $id_2 < id − 1$, id_2, id_3. Process p_2 sees that $p = 4$ processes have accessed the splitter $SM[4, 1, \text{up}]$, and consequently computes *last* $= 1 + (2 \times 4 - 2) = 7$. The size of its new name space is $[1..2p - 1] = [1..7]$. As it does not have the greatest initial name among the four processes, p_2 invokes new_name$(3, 6, \text{down}, id_2)$, and recursively new_name$(2, 6, \text{down})$ and new_name$(1, 6, \text{down}, id - 2)$, and finally obtains 6 as its new name.

3.6   CONCLUSION

The aim of this chapter was to be an introductory tutorial on concurrency-related recursion in asynchronous read/write systems where any number of processes may crash. The chapter has shown that a new type of recursion is introduced by the net effect of asynchrony and failures, namely the recursion parameter is used to allow a process to learn the number of processes with which it has to coordinate to compute its local result. This recursion has been illustrated with two task examples: write-snapshot and adaptive renaming. Interestingly, the first example is related to a linear time notion, while the second one is related to a branching time notion.

CHAPTER 4

The BG Simulation

Considering the asynchronous read/write system model in which all the processes except one can crash, namely the system model $\mathcal{CARW}_{n,t}[t = n - 1]$, the BG simulation is a distributed algorithm that allows a set of $n = t + 1$ processes to simulate the execution of an algorithm executed by $m \geq t + 1$ processes that tolerates up to t process crash failures. So, the BG simulation is a conceptual tool that can be used to prove the solvability or the unsolvability of distributed problems (named distributed tasks). As a simple example, if a task T is unsolvable in $\mathcal{CARW}_{n,t}[t = n - 1]$, it remains unsolvable in $\mathcal{CARW}_{m,t}[m \geq t + 1]$. Stated differently, increasing the number of correct processes does not increase the computability power as far as the task T is concerned.

Keywords: Arbiter, Asynchronous processes, BG simulation, Colorless task, Colored task, Distributed computability, Distributed task, Fault-tolerance, Mutual exclusion, Process crash, Read/write shared memory system, Reduction algorithm, t-Resilience, System model, Wait-freedom.

4.1   INTRODUCTION

The BG simulation has been introduced in 1993 by E. Borowsky and E. Gafni [22] (hence its name). It has been formally proved correct in [24]. A short introduction can be found in [118].

The BG simulation is a distributed algorithm that allows a system of n asynchronous processes that solve a distributed task despite the crash of up to $t = n - 1$ processes, to simulate a system of $m \geq n$ asynchronous processes that solve the same task despite the crash of up to $t = n - 1$ processes as described in Figure 4.1. As far as notations are concerned, n denotes the number of simulator processes, m denotes the number of simulated processes, and t denotes both the maximal number of simulated processes that can crash, and the maximal number of simulator processes that can crash.

BG simulation: why?   The important lesson learned from the BG simulation is that in a crash failure-prone distributed computing model, the critical model parameter is not the total number of processes but the maximal number of processes that may crash.

As an example, let us consider the k-set agreement problem in which each process proposes a value, each process that does not crash must decide a proposed value, and at most k different values can be decided. Let us notice that the 1-set agreement problem is the consensus

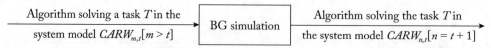

Figure 4.1: What the BG simulation does.

problem. It has been shown in $[22, 75, 128]^1$ that the k-set agreement problem is impossible to solve in the system model $CARW_{n,t}[n = k + 1, t = k]$.

Let us assume by contradiction that there is an algorithm A that allows k-set agreement to be solved for any $m \geq k + 1$ processes among which $t = k$ may crash (system model $CARW_{m,t}[m \geq k + 1, t = k]$). The BG simulation of A in the system model $CARW_{n,t}[n = k + 1, t = k]$ shows that, as k-set agreement cannot be solved in $CARW_{n,t}[n = k + 1, t = k]$, it cannot be solved either in the system model $CARW_{m,t}[m \geq k + 1, t = k]$.

Content of the chapter   The chapter is divided into three sections. The first is a reminder on the notion of distributed tasks. The second presents the a BG simulation algorithm for colorless tasks, while the third one presents the a BG simulation simulation algorithm for colored tasks.

4.2   DISTRIBUTED TASK

4.2.1   NOTION OF A TASK

The problems we are interested in are called *distributed tasks*.[2] These tasks capture coordination problems in which each process has an input value, and must communicate with the other processes to compute an output value. Using a classical terminology, in every execution each process proposes a value and the proposed values define an input vector I where $I[j]$ is the value proposed by p_j. Let $\mathcal{I}$ denote the set of allowed input vectors. Each process has to decide a value. The decided values define an output vector O, such that $O[j]$ is the value decided by p_j. Let $\mathcal{O}$ be the set of the output vectors. A task is defined by a binary relation Δ from $\mathcal{I}$ into $\mathcal{O}$, hence a task T is a triple $(\Delta, \mathcal{I}, \mathcal{O})$. There are two types of tasks.

- A task is *colorless* if, when a value v is decided by a process p_j (i.e., $O[j] = v$), then that value v can be decided by any other process. Consensus, and more generally k-set agreement, are colorless tasks.

- A task is *colored* if, when a value v is decided by a process p_j (i.e., $O[j] = v$), then v cannot be decided by another process. Renaming $[10, 22, 31]$ is a colored task (the input value of a process is its initial name, its output is its new name).[3]

---

[1] These three articles have open the door of the topology-based approach to model executions in the distributed computing model $CARW_{n,t}[n > t, t]$. The interested reader can also consult $[68, 72, 73]$.

[2] A formal presentation of decision tasks can be found in the literature, e.g., $[4, 24, 53, 75]$.

[3] Reminder: the feasibility of the renaming task depends on the size M allowed for the new name space. In the system model $CARW_{n,t}[n = t + 1]$ renaming is possible for $M \geq 2n - 1$, otherwise it is impossible $[10, 30, 75]$.

4.2.2   ALGORITHM SOLVING A TASK

An algorithm solves a task T in the n-process t-resilient model $(CARW_{n,t}[t < n]$ if, given any $I \in \mathcal{I}$, each correct process p_j decides a value o_j and there is an output vector O such that $(I, O) \in \Delta$ where O is defined as follows:

- if p_j decides v, then $\mathcal{O}[j] = v$ and

- if (because it crashed) p_j does not decide, $O[j]$ is set to any value v' that preserves the relation $(I, O) \in \Delta$.

A task is solvable in a model if there is an algorithm that solves it in that model. As an example, consensus is not solvable in the model $CARW_{n,t}[t = 1]$ [50, 97]. Differently, renaming where the size of the new name space is $(2n - 1)$ is solvable in the model $CARW_{n,t}[t < n]$ environment [10, 15, 75].

4.3   BG SIMULATION: PRELIMINARIES

4.3.1   NOTATION

Let A be an m-process algorithm that solves a task in the model $CARW_{m,t}[t < m]$. The aim is to design an algorithm A' that simulates A in $CARW_{n,t}[n = t + 1]$. The reader is referred to [24] for a formal definition of a simulation.[4]

A simulated process (in short "process") is denoted p_j with $1 \leq j \leq m$, and the subscript j is always used to refer to a simulated process. Similarly, a simulator process (in short "simulator") is denoted q_i with $1 \leq i \leq n = t + 1$, and the subscript i is always used to refer to a simulator.

4.3.2   SWMR SNAPSHOT-BASED COMMUNICATION

It is assumed that the processes cooperate through a SWMR snapshot memory $mem[1..m]$, which means that:

- only process p_j can write $mem[j]$ and

- the operation $mem.\text{snapshot}()$ allows any process p_i to read the full memory $mem[1..m]$.

The snapshot object is SWMR because, while each entry of the array can read by all the processes, it can be written only by a single predefined process.

The two previous operations are atomic, which means that they appear as being executed instantaneously at different points of the time line of an omniscient external observer in such a way that, if op1 is terminated before op2 starts, op1 appears before op2. The resulting sequence of operations is called a linearization of the snapshot object, and we say that the operations are linearized.

Distributed algorithms implementing a SWMR snapshot memory in the presence of any number of process crashes are described in [1, 7].

---

[4]An intuitive presentation of the BG simulation is given in [127].

4.3.3   SIMULATED PROCESSES VS. SIMULATOR PROCESSES

Notation   As far the objects accessed by the simulators are concerned, the following convention is adopted. The objects denoted with upper case letters are the objects shared by the simulators. Differently, an object denoted with lower case letters is local to a simulator (in that case, the associated subscript denotes the corresponding simulator).

What a simulator does   Each simulator q_i is given the code and the input values of all the simulated processes $p_1, \ldots, p_m$. It manages m threads, each one associated with a simulated process, and locally executes these threads in a fair way. It also manages a local copy mem_i of the snapshot memory mem shared by the simulated processes $p_1, \ldots, p_m$. Each simulator can have its own scheduling of the simulated processes.

The code of a simulated process p_j contains writes of $mem[j]$ and invocations of mem.snapshot(). These are the only operations used by the processes $p_1, \ldots, p_n$ to cooperate. So, the core of the simulation is the definition of two algorithms. The first (denoted cll_sim_write$_{i,j}$()) has to describe what a simulator q_i has to do in order to correctly simulate a write of $mem[j]$ issued by a process p_j. The second (denoted clr_sim_snapshot$_{i,j}$()) has to describe what a simulator q_i has to do in order to correctly simulate an invocation of mem.snapshot() issued by a process p_j.

4.4   BASE OBJECT USED IN BOTH SIMULATIONS: safe_agreement

4.4.1   THE safe_agreement OBJECT TYPE

In addition to snapshot objects (as the simulated processes), the simulators also cooperate through atomic read/write register objects, and a specific object type denoted safe_agreement. This object type can be implemented from multi reader/multi writer atomic registers despite any number of simulator crashes.

This object type, defined in [22], is at the core of the BG simulation. It provides each simulator q_i with two operations, denoted propose$_i(v)$ and decide$_i()$, that q_i can invoke at most once, and in that order. The operation propose$_i(v)$ allows q_i to propose a value v while decide$_i()$ allows it to decide a value. The properties defining an object of the type safe_agreement are the following.

- Termination. If no simulator q_x crashes while executing propose$_x()$, then any correct simulator q_i that invokes decide$_i()$, returns from its invocation.

- Agreement. At most one value is decided.

- Validity. A decided value is a proposed value.

4.4.2   AN ALGORITHM IMPLEMENTING THE safe_agreement TYPE

Algorithm 4.1 (due to [24]) implements the safe_agreement object type. This construction is based on a snapshot object SM (with one entry per simulator q_i). Each entry $SM[i]$ of the snapshot object has two fields: $SM[i].value$ that contains a value and $SM[i].level$ that stores its level. The level 0 means the corresponding value is meaningless, 1 means it is unstable, while 2 means it is stable.

Algorithm 4.1 An algorithm implementing the safe_agreement type (code for q_i)

---

init: for each $x : 1 \leq x \leq t + 1$ **do** $SM[x] \leftarrow (\perp, 0)$ **end for.**

operation propose$_i$ (v) **is**   % code for simulator q_i, $1 \leq i \leq t + 1$ %
(1) $SM[i] \leftarrow (v, 1)$;
(2) $sm_i \leftarrow SM$.snapshot();
(3)   **if** $(\exists x : sm_i[x].level = 2)$ **then** $SM[i] \leftarrow (v, 0)$ **else** $SM[i] \leftarrow (v, 2)$ **end if;**
(4)   return()
end of operation.

operation decide$_i$ () **is**
(5)   **repeat** $sm_i \leftarrow SM$.snapshot() **until** $(\forall x : sm_i[x].level \neq 1)$ **end repeat;**
(6) $res_i \leftarrow sm_i[x].value$ where $x = \min(\{k \mid sm_i[k].level = 2\})$;
(7)   return(res_i)
end of operation.

When a simulator q_i invokes propose$_i$ (v), it first writes the pair $(v, 1)$ in $SM[i]$ (line 1), and then reads the snapshot object SM (line 2). If there is a stable value in SM, p_i "cancels" the value it proposes, otherwise it makes it stable (line 3).

A simulator q_i invokes decide$_i$ () after it has invoked propose$_i$ (). Its aim is to return the same stable value to all the simulators that invoke this operation (line 7). To that end, q_i repeatedly computes a snapshot of SM until it sees no unstable value in SM (line 5). Let us observe that, as a simulator q_i invokes decide$_i$ () after it has invoked propose$_i$ (v), there is at least one stable value in SM when it executes line 6. Finally, in order that the same stable value be returned to all, q_i returns the stable value proposed by the simulator with the smallest id (line 6).

4.4.3   PROOF OF THE SAFE-AGREEMENT ALGORITHM

Lemma 4.1   *A single value is returned by invocations of* decide$_i$ ().

Proof As snapshot objects are linearizable, it is possible to associate a date with each snapshot operation, no two operations having the same date. Let t be the date of the first snapshot operation that returns an array sm_i containing an entry k such that $sm_i[k].level = 2$. This snapshot operation was invoked by a simulator q_i either in a propose$_i$ () or decide$_i$ () operation.

Any simulator q_i that takes a snapshot during its $\mathsf{propose}_j()$ operation after date t will not set its level at 2 (line 5). Thus, the set of simulators $\{q_k | SM[k].level = 2\}$ will not change after date t, and no simulator will get out of the loop at lines 6–7 before taking a snapshot after t. So, no two processes return different values. $\square_{Lemma\ 4.1}$

Lemma 4.2   *If no simulator q_i crashes while it executes the $\mathsf{propose}_i()$ operation, all the correct simulators p_x terminate their invocation of $\mathsf{decide}_x()$.*

Proof For any simulator q_i, before and after its invocation of $\mathsf{propose}_i()$, we have $SM[i].level \neq 1$. Moreover, the loop at line 5 is repeated only if $\exists j : SM[j].level = 1$. Thus, if no simulator crashes during an invocation of $\mathsf{propose}_x()$, all the correct processes terminate their invocation of $\mathsf{decide}_x()$. $\square_{Lemma\ 4.2}$

Lemma 4.3   *The decided value is a proposed value.*

Proof If an invocation of $\mathsf{decide}_i()$ terminates and returns a value, it returns a value that it has obtained through a snapshot at line 5, and such a value has been written at line 1. It follows that it is a proposed value. $\square_{Lemma\ 4.3}$

Theorem 4.4   *Algorithm 4.1 implements the safe-agreement object type.*

Proof The proof follows directly from the previous lemmas. $\square_{Theorem\ 4.4}$

4.5   BG SIMULATION FOR COLORLESS TASKS

This section presents the BG simulation for colorless tasks [22, 24]: its main principles and algorithms implementing its base operations $\mathsf{sim\_write}_{i,j}()$ and $\mathsf{sim\_snapshot}_{i,j}()$. A formal proof of it (based on input/output automata) is presented [24].

4.5.1   THE MEMORY $MEM[1..(t+1)]$ SHARED BY THE SIMULATORS

The snapshot memory *mem* shared by the (simulated) processes $p_1, \ldots, p_m$ is emulated by a snapshot object MEM shared by the simulators (so, MEM has $(t+1)$ entries). More specifically, $MEM[i]$ is an atomic register that contains an array with one entry per simulated process p_j. Each $MEM[i][j]$ is made up of two fields: a field $MEM[i][j].value$ that contains the last value of $mem[j]$ written by the (simulated) process p_j, and a field $MEM[i][j].sn$ that contains an associated sequence number (this sequence number, introduced by the simulation, is a control data that will be used to produce a consistent simulation of the $mem.\mathsf{snapshot}()$ operations issued by the simulated processes p_j).

4.5.2   ALGORITHM IMPLEMENTING THE sim_write$_{i,j}$() OPERATION

Algorithm 4.2 describes the implementation of sim_write$_{i,j}(v)$, executed by q_i to simulate the write by p_j of the value v into $mem[j]$. Its code is pretty simple. The simulator q_i first increases a local sequence number $w\_sn_i[j]$ that will be associated with the value v written by p_j into $mem[j]$. Then, q_i writes the pair $\langle v, w\_sn_i[j] \rangle$ into $mem_i[j]$ (where mem_i is its local copy of the memory shared by the simulated processes) and finally writes atomically its local copy mem_i into $MEM[i]$.

Algorithm 4.2 write$_{i,j}(v)$ executed by q_i to simulate write(v) issued by p_j.

---

operation sim_write$_{i,j}(v)$ **is**
(1) $w\_sn_i[j] \leftarrow w\_sn_i[j] + 1$;
(2) $mem_i[j] \leftarrow \langle v, w\_sn_i[j] \rangle$;
(3) $MEM[i] \leftarrow mem_i$
end of operation.

4.5.3   ALGORITHM IMPLEMENTING THE cll_sim_snapshot$_{i,j}$() OPERATION

Algorithm 4.3 describes the implementation of the operation cll_sim_snapshot$_{i,j}$() when it is invoked by a simulator q_i to simulate the snapshot operation issued by the simulated process p_j.

Additional local and shared objects   For each process p_j, a simulator q_i manages a local sequence number generator $snap\_sn_i[j]$ used to associates a sequence number with each mem.snapshot() it simulates on behalf of p_j (line 6).

In addition to the snapshot object $MEM[1..(t + 1)]$, the simulators $q_1, \ldots, q_{t+1}$ cooperate through an array $SAFE\_AG[1..n, 0 \ldots]$ of safe_agreement type objects.

Underlying principle of the BG simulation: obtain a consistent value   In order to agree on the very same output of the *snapshot*-th invocation of mem.snapshot() issued by p_j, the set of simulators $q_1, \ldots, q_{t+1}$ cooperate through the shared object $SAFE\_AG[j, snapsn]$.

Each simulator q_i proposes a value (denoted $input_i$) to that object (line 8) and, due to its agreement property, that object will deliver them the same output at line 10. In order to ensure the consistent progress of the simulation, the input value $input_i$ proposed by the simulator q_i to $SAFE\_AG[j, snapsn]$ is defined as follows.

- First, q_i issues a snapshot of MEM in order to obtain a consistent view of the simulation state. The value of this snapshot is kept in sm_i (line 1).

  Let us observe that $sm_i[x][y]$ is such that (1) $sm_i[x][y].sn$ is the number of writes issues by p_y into $mem[y]$ that have been simulated up to now by q_x, and (2) $sm_i[x][y].value$ is the value of the last write into $mem[y]$ as simulated by q_x on behalf of p_y.

- Then, for each p_y, q_i computes $input_i[y]$. To that end, it extracts from $sm_i[1..t+1][y]$ the value written by the more advanced simulator q_s as far as the simulation of p_y is concerned. This is expressed in lines 2–5.

Algorithm 4.3 cll_sim_snapshot$_{i,j}$() executed by q_i to simulate mem.snapshot() issued by p_j.

```
operation cll_sim_snapshot_{i,j}() is
(1)      sm_i ← MEM.snapshot():
(2)      for each y ∈ {1,...,m} do
(3)           input_i[y] ← sm_i[s][y].value where s is such that
(4)               ∀x ∈ {1,...,t+1} sm_i[s][y].sn ≥ sm_i[x][y].sn
(5)      end for;
(6)      snap_sn_i[j] ← snap_sn_i[j] + 1; let snapsn = snap_sn_i[j];
(7)      acquire();
(8)         SAFE_AG[j, snapsn].propose_i(input_i);
(9)      release();
(10)     res_i ← SAFE_AG[j, snapsn].decide_i();
(11)     return(res_i)
end of operation.
```

Once, $input_i$ has been computed, q_i proposes it to $SAFE\_AG[j, snapsn]$ (line 8), and then returns the value decided by that object (lines 10–11).

The previous description shows an important feature of the BG simulation. A value $input_i[y] = sm_i[s][y].value$ proposed by a simulator q_i can be such that $sm_i[s][y].sn > sm_i[i][y].sn$, i.e., the simulator q_s is more advanced than q_i as far as the simulation of p_y is concerned. This causes no problem, as when q_i will simulate mem.snapshot() operations for p_y (if any) that are between the $(sm_i[i][y].sn)$-th and the $(sm_i[s][y].sn)$-th write operations of p_y, it will obtain a value that has already been computed and is currently kept in the corresponding $SAFE\_AG[y, -]$ object.

Underlying principle of the BG simulation: from a simulator crash to a single process crash
Each simulator q_i simulates the m processes $p_1, \ldots, p_m$ "in parallel" and in a fair way. But any simulator q_i can crash. The crash of q_i while it is engaged in the simulation of mem.snapshot() on behalf of several processes p_j, $p_{j'}$, etc., can entail their definitive blocking, i.e., their crash. This is because each $SAFE\_AG[j, -]$ object guarantees that its $SAFE\_AG[j, -]$.decide() invocations do terminate only if no simulator crashes while executing $SAFE\_AG[j, -]$.propose() (line 8 of Figure 4.3).

The simple (and nice) idea of the BG simulation to solve this problem consists in allowing a simulator to be engaged in only one $SAFE\_AG[-, -]$.propose() invocation at a time. Hence, if the simulator q_i crashes while executing $SAFE\_AG[j, -]$.propose(), it can entails the crash of p_j only. This is obtained by using an additional mutual exclusion object offering the operations acquire() and release() [43]. (Let us notice that such a mutex object is purely local to each simulator: it solves conflicts among the simulating threads inside each simulator, and has nothing to do with the memory shared by the simulators.)

Example   As an example let us consider we have an algorithm that solves the t-agreement problem in $\mathcal{CARW}_{n,t}[\emptyset]$. Each simulator q_i ($1 \leq i \leq t + 1$) is initially given a proposed value v_i, and the base objects $SAFE\_AG[1, \ldots, m, 0]$ are used by the $(t + 1)$ simulators as follows to determine the value proposed by p_j. For each j, $1 \leq j \leq n$, the simulator q_i invokes first $SAFE\_AG[j, 0].\text{propose}_i(v_i)$ and then $SAFE\_AG[j, 0].\text{decide}_i()$ that returns it a value that it considers as the value proposed by p_j. It is easy to see that, for any j, all the simulators obtain the same value for p_j. Moreover, this value is one of the $(t + 1)$ values proposed by the simulators. Finally, a simulator process q_i can decide any of the values decided by the processes p_j it is simulating.

From wait-freedom to t-resilience   For colorless decision tasks, t-resilience can easily be reduced to wait-freedom as follows. First, each application process deposits its input value in a shared register. Then, every process of the $(t + 1)$ processes of the wait-free algorithm takes one of those values as its input value and executes its code. Finally, each application process decides any value decided by a process of the wait-free algorithm.

4.6   BG SIMULATION FOR COLORED TASKS

This section presents a BG simulation algorithm for colored tasks introduced in [78]. This simulation is similar to the simulation for colored tasks, except for the simulation of the operation sim_snapshot$_{i,j}()$, which is replaced by the clr_sim_snapshot$_{i,j}()$.

4.6.1   FROM COLORLESS TASKS TO COLORED TASKS

Colorless tasks are symmetric in the sense that a value is decided by a process can also be decided by any other process, while colored tasks are asymmetric in the sense that the value decided by a process is specific to that process.

On the BG implementation side, the core of the BG simulation relies on the following principles: (1) each of the $(t + 1)$ simulators fairly simulates all the processes, and this simulation is such that (2) the crash of a simulator entails the crash of at most one simulated process. The BG simulation is symmetric in the sense that each of the m processes is simulated by every simulator and the $(t + 1)$ simulators are equal with respect to each simulated process. One way to be able to simulate colored tasks (without preventing the simulation of colorless tasks) consists in introducing some form of asymmetry in the BG algorithm.

The BG simulation for colored tasks presented below realizes the appropriate asymmetry as follows. While (as in the base BG simulation) a simulator q_i simulates all the processes, it is now associated with exactly one simulated process p_j, such that no two simulated processes are associated with a same simulator. We say that the simulator q_i is the owner of the simulated process p_j. The ownership notion is used to to ensure that the corresponding simulated process p_j will not be blocked forever (perceived as crashed) if its owner simulator q_i does not crash. Hence, if a simulator does not crash, it can always decide the value decided by the simulated process p_j it owns.

4.6.2   A NEW OBJECT TYPE: arbiter

Definition   Each object of the type arbiter has a statically predefined owner simulator q_j. Such an object provides the simulators with a single operation denoted arbitrate$_{i,j}$() (where i is the identity of the invoking simulator and j the identity of the owner). A simulator q_i invokes arbitrate$_{i,j}$() at most once, and, when it terminates, this invocation returns a value to q_i. The properties of an object of the type arbiter owned by q_j are the following where it is assumed (without loss of generality) that q_i owns p_i.

- Termination. If the owner q_j invokes arbitrate$_{j,j}$() and is correct, or does not invoke arbitrate$_{j,j}$(), or if a simulator q_i returns from its invocation arbitrate$_{i,j}$(), then all the correct simulators return from their arbitrate$_{i,j}$() invocation.

- Agreement. No two processes return different values.

- Validity. The returned value is 1 (owner) or 0 (not_owner). Moreover, if the owner does not invoke arbitrate$_{j,j}$(), 1 cannot be returned, and if only the owner invokes arbitrate$_{j,j}$(), 0 cannot be returned.

An implementation   Algorithm 4.4 describes the implementation of an object of the type arbiter. It is based on an underlying snapshot object *PART* (initialized to [false, $\cdots$, false]), and a multi-writer/multi-reader atomic register *WINNER* (initialized to $\perp$).

When it invokes arbitrate$_{i,j}$(), the simulator q_i announces that it participates (line 1), and issues a snapshot to know the simulators that are currently participating (line 2). If q_i is the owner of the object ($i = j$, line 3), it checks if it is the first participant (predicate $part_i = \{i\}$). If it is, it sets *WINNER* to 1, otherwise it sets it to 0 (line 4). If q_i is not the owner of the object ($i \neq j$), it checks if the owner is a participating simulator (predicate $j \in part_i$). If it is, q_i waits to know which value has been assigned to *WINNER*. If it is not, it sets *WINNER* to 0. Finally, q_i terminates by returning the value of *WINNER*.

4.6.3   PROOF OF THE arbiter OBJECT TYPE

Lemma 4.5   *If the owner simulator participates and is correct, all correct participating simulators terminate. If the owner simulator does not participate, all correct participating simulators terminate. If a simulator terminates, all correct participating simulators terminate.*

Proof Let us first consider the case where the owner simulator participates and is correct. There is no loop and the only blocking statement of the algorithm is the wait statement at line 5 where

Algorithm 4.4 The arbitrate$_{i,j}$() operation of the arbiter object type (code for q_i)

```
operation arbitrate_{i,j}() is    % 1 ≤ i, j ≤ t + 1 %
(1)        PART[i] ← true;
(2)        aux_i ← PART.snapshot(); part_i ← {x | aux_i[x]};
(3)        if (i = j)    % p_i is the owner of the associated arbiter type object %
(4)            then if (part_i = {i}) then WINNER ← 1 else WINNER ← 0 end if
(5)            else  if (j ∈ part_i) then wait (WINNER ≠ ⊥) else WINNER ← 0 end if
(6)        end if;
(7)        return(WINNER)
end of operation.
```

a simulator q_i waits for a value to be assigned to *WINNER*. The owner simulator (q_j) always assigns a value (1 or 0) to *WINNER* before it terminates (line 4). So, if the owner participates and is correct, no correct participating simulator can be blocked forever at line 5 and consequently terminates.

Let us now consider the case where the owner simulator does not participate. Again, the only possible blocking statement is the wait statement at line 5. This statement is executed by a simulator only if it observes that the owner simulator has started participating (predicate $j \in part_i$). So, if the owner does not participate, all correct participating simulators terminate.

Let us finally consider the case where a simulator terminates.

It follows from line 5 that, if a simulator terminates it previously found *WINNER* $\neq \perp$, i.e., *WINNER* $\in \{0, 1\}$. So, if a simulator terminates, all correct participating simulators terminate.

$\square$*Lemma* 4.5

Lemma 4.6 *No two simulator return different values. If the owner simulator does not participate, the value returned is* 0. *If the owner simulator participates alone, the value returned is* 1.

Proof Let us first show that no two simulator return different values. The only simulator that can assign a value different from 0 to *WINNER* is the owner (line 4). So, we only have to consider this case. If the owner assigns the value 1 to *WINNER*, it means that, in the snapshot it has taken at line 2, it did not observe any other simulator (line 4). Because snapshots are linearizable and the owner announced that it started before taking the snapshot (line 1), all the other simulators will see that the owner has started and will execute the wait statement (line 5) instead of assigning 0 to *WINNER*. Thus, all simulators return the same value.

Let us now consider the case where the owner simulator does not participate. The only simulator that can assign a value different from 0 to *WINNER* is the owner (line 4). So, if the owner does not participate, the value of *WINNER* is 0, and the other simulators return this value.

Let us finally consider the case where the owner simulator participates alone. If the owner does not observe any other participating simulator, it assigns the value 1 to *WINNER*. Hence, if the owner participates alone, it returns 1.

$\square$*Lemma* 4.6

Theorem 4.7   *Algorithm* 4.4 *implements the* arbiter *object type.*

Proof The proof follows from the Lemmas 4.5–4.6. $\square_{Theorem}$ 4.7

4.6.4   ADDITIONAL SHARED OBJECTS

In addition to *MEM* and *SAFE_AG*[$1..m, 0...$], the memory shared by the simulators $q_1, \ldots, q_{t+1}$ contains the following objects.

- *ARBITER*[$1..t + 1, 0...$] is an array of arbiter objects. The objects contained in *ARBITER*[$j, -$] are owned by the simulator q_j ($1 \leq j \leq t + 1$).

  The object *ARBITER*[$j, snapsn$] is used by a simulator q_i when it simulates its *snapsn*-th invocation *mem*.snapshot() on behalf of the simulated process p_j for $1 \leq j \leq t + 1$. (As we will see, when $t + 1 < j \leq m$, the simulation of *mem*.snapshot() on behalf of p_j does not require the help of an arbiter object.)

- *ARB_VAL*[$1..t + 1, 0...$][$0..1$] is an array of pairs of atomic registers. The pair of atomic registers *ARB_VAL*[$j, snapsn$][$0..1$] is used in conjunction with the arbiter object *ARBITER*[$j, snapsn$].

  The aim of *ARB_VAL*[$j, snapsn$][1] is to contain the value that has to be returned to the *snapsn*-th invocation *mem*.snapshot(), on behalf of the simulated process p_j, if the owner q_j is designated as the winner by the associated object *ARBITER*[$j, snapsn$]. If the owner q_j is not the winner, the value that has to be returned is the one kept in *ARB_VAL*[$j, snapsn$][0].

4.6.5   ALGORITHM IMPLEMENTING THE clr_sim_snapshot$_{i,j}$() OPERATION

The algorithm   Algorithm 4.5 implements the operation clr_sim_snapshot$_{i,j}$() which is executed by q_i to simulate a *mem*.snapshot() operation issued by p_j. Its first four lines and its last line are exactly the same as in Figure 4.3. Lines 10–11 are replaced by the new lines N01–N14 that constitute the "addition" that allows going from the BG to the extended BG simulation.

Underlying principle   Albeit each simulated process p_j ($1 \leq j \leq m$) is simulated by each simulator q_i ($1 \leq i \leq t + 1$) as in the colorless BG simulation, each simulated process p_j such that $1 \leq j \leq t + 1$ is associated with exactly one simulator that is its "owner": q_i is the owner of p_j if $j = i$ (and also the owner of the corresponding objects *ARBITER*[$j, -$]). The aim is, for any *snapsn* ≥ 0, to associate a single returned value with the *snapsn*-th invocations of e_sim_snapshot$_{i,j}$() issued by the simulators. The idea is to use the ownership notion to "short-cut" the use of *SAFE_AG*[$j, snapsn$] object in appropriate circumstances.

Algorithm 4.5 clr_sim_snapshot$_{i,j}$() executed by q_i to simulate *mem.snapshot*() issued by p_j

```
operation clr_sim_snapshot_{i,j}() is
(1)        sm_i ← MEM.snapshot():
(2)        for each y ∈ {1,...,m} input_i[y] = sm_i[s, y].value do
(3)            input_i[y] ← sm_i[s][y].value where s is such that
(4)                ∀x ∈ {1,...,t + 1} sm_i[s][y].sn ≥ sm_i[x][y].sn
(5)        end for;
(6)        snap_sn_i[j] ← snap_sn_i[j] + 1; let snapsn = snap_sn_i[j];
(N01)      if (j > t + 1)
(N02)          then acquire(); SAFE_AG[j, snapsn].propose_i(input_i); release();
(N03)              res_i ← SAFE_AG[j, snapsn].decide_i()
(N04)          else if (i = j)
(N05)                  then ARB_VAL[j, snapsn][1] ← input_i;
(N06)                      acquire(); win ← ARBITER[j, snapsn].arbitrate_{i,j}(); release();
(N07)                      if (win = 1) then res ← input_i
(N08)                          else res_i ← ARB_VAL[j, snapsn][0] end if
(N09)                  else acquire(); SAFE_AG[j, snapsn].propose(input_i); release();
(N10)                      ARB_VAL[j, snapsn][0] ← SAFE_AG[j, snapsn].decide_i();
(N11)                      r ← ARBITER[j, snapsn].arbitrate_{i,j}();
(N12)                      res ← ARB_VAL[j, snapsn][r]
(N13)                  end if
(N14)          end if;
(11)       return(res_i)
end of operation.
```

The operation clr_sim_snapshot$_{i,j}$() for the simulated processes p_j such that $t + 2 \leq j \leq m$, is exactly the same as sim_snapshot$_{i,j}$(). This appears in lines N02–N03 that are the same as lines 10–11 of Figure 4.3 (in that case, there is no ownership notion).

The new lines N04-N14 address the case of the simulated processes owned by simulators, i.e., the processes $p_1, \ldots, p_{t+1}$. The idea is the following: if q_i does not crash, p_i must not crash. In that way, if q_i is correct, p_i will always terminate whatever the behavior of the other simulators. To that end, q_i on one side, and all the other simulators on the other side, compete to define the snapshot value returned by the *snapsn*-th invocations clr_sim_snapshot$_{i,j}$() issued by each of them. To attain this goal, the additional objects $ARBITER[j, snapsn]$ and $ARB\_VAL[j, snapsn]$ are used as follows.

All the simulators invoke $ARBITER[j, snapsn].$arbitrate$_{i,j}$() (at line N06 if q_i is the owner, and line N11 if it is not). According to the specification of the arbiter type, these invocations do not return different values and do return at least when the owner q_j is correct and invokes that operation (as indicated in the specification, there are other cases where the invocations do terminate). Finally, the value returned indicates if the winner is the owner (1) or not (0).

- If the winner is the owner q_j, the value returned by the *snapsn*-th invocations of clr_sim_snapshot$_{i,j}$() (one invocation by simulator) is the value $input_j$ computed by the owner. That value is kept in the atomic register $ARB\_VAL[j, snapsn][1]$ (line N05).

- If the owner is not the winner, the value returned is the one determined by the other simulators that invoked $SAFE\_AG[j, snapsn].\mathsf{propose}_i(input_i)$ (line N09) and $SAFE\_AG[j, snapsn].\mathsf{decide}_i()$ (line N10). The value they have computed has been deposited in $ARB\_VAL[j, snapsn][0]$ (line N10), and this value is used as the result of the $SAFE\_AG[j, snapsn]$ object.

It is important to notice that the owner q_j does not invoke the $\mathsf{propose}_j()$ and $\mathsf{decide}_j()$ operations on the objects it owns. Moreover, the simulator q_j is the only simulator that can write $ARB\_VAL[j, snapsn][1]$, while the other simulators can write only in $ARB\_VAL[j, snapsn][0]$.

To summarize, if a simulator q_i crashes, it entails the crash of at most one simulated process. This is ensured thanks to the mutex algorithm. If the simulator q_i crashes, $1 \le i \le t + 1$, as far the simulated processes are concerned, it can entail either no crash at all (if q_i crashes outside a critical section), or the crash of p_i (if it crashes while executing $\mathsf{arbitrate}_{i,j}()$ inside the critical section at line N06), or the crash of a process p_j such that $1 \le j \ne i \le t + 1$ (this can occur only if q_j has crashed and was not winner, and q_i crashes inside the critical section at line N09), or the crash of one of the processes $p_{t+2}, \ldots, p_m$ (if it crashes at line N02 inside the critical section).

4.6.6   PROOF OF THE COLORED BG SIMULATION

Lemma 4.8   *A simulator can block the progression of only one simulated process at a time.*

Proof A simulator can block the simulation of a process only during the execution of the clr_sim_snapshot() operation, when the simulator accesses a safe_agreement object (lines N02–N03 or N09–N10) or an arbiter object because it is its owner (line N06). All these invocations are placed in mutual exclusion. Thus, a simulator can block the simulation of only a single process at a time. $\square_{Lemma\ 4.8}$

Lemma 4.9   *If the simulator q_i does not crash, the progress of the simulated process p_i is never blocked at the simulator q_i.*

Proof When invoked by the simulator q_i for the simulated process p_i (line N04, $i = j$), the operation clr_sim_snapshot() does not include any wait statement and does not use a safe_agreement object. Due to the properties of the arbiter object type, it cannot be blocked during its invocation of $\mathsf{arbitrate}_{i,i}()$. Thus, the simulated process p_i can never be blocked at simulator q_i. $\square_{Lemma\ 4.9}$

Lemma 4.10   *Each simulator receives the decision values of at least $(m - t)$ simulated processes.*

Proof Because at most t simulators may crash, and a simulator can block at most one simulated process at a time (Lemma 4.8), each simulator can execute the code of at least $(m - t)$ simulated processes without being blocked forever. Hence, $(m - t)$ processes will decide a value.

$\square$*Lemma* 4.10

Lemma 4.11   *All the simulators that return from the simulation of the k-th snapshot issued by the simulated process p_j return the same snapshot value.*

Proof If p_j is not owned by a simulator $(j > t + 1)$, because of the properties of the safe_agreement objects, the same value is always returned (lines N02–N03 of Figure 4.5).

If the simulator q_j owner of p_j chooses the value it has computed for p_j's k-th snapshot, it has written this value in $ARB\_VAL[j, snapsn][1]$ (line N05), and is the winner of the arbiter object (line N06). All other simulators will then read its value (line N12).

If the simulated process p_j has an owner but another process chooses the value it has computed for p_j's k-th snapshot, this process has already agreed on a value with all other non-owner simulated processes (safe_agreement object, lines N09–N10) and is the winner of the arbiter object (lines N11–N12). All non-owner processes will then write the same value in $ARB\_VAL[j, snapsn][0]$ (line N10) and the owner will read it (line N08).

Thus, all the simulators that return a value for the k-th snapshot of the simulated process p_j return the same value.

$\square$*Lemma* 4.11

Lemma 4.12   *At most one decision value can be decided by a simulated process on any simulator.*

Proof Because every simulator computes the same value for any given snapshot and because the snapshot operations are the only non-deterministic parts of codes of the simulated processes, all simulators that decide a value for a given simulated process decide the same value.

$\square$*Lemma* 4.12

Lemma 4.13   *The sequences of all write and snapshot operations for each simulated process correspond to a correct execution of the simulated algorithm.*

Proof Every simulator that is not blocked while simulating a process simulates it in the same way (same values written and same snapshots read, Lemma 4.11).

When simulator q_i executes e_sim_snapshot() for p_j (i.e., the simulation of a snapshot for p_j), it stores in its $input_i$ variable the values written by the simulators that have advanced the most for each simulated process (Figure 4.2 and lines 1–3 of Figure 4.5). It can choose its own $input_i$ snapshot value only if no other simulator has already ended the execution of this e_sim_snapshot() (Lemma 4.11 implies that safe_agreement objects have a "memory" effect). Thus, for each e_sim_snapshot(), q_i returns an $input$ value computed by itself or another simulator. Let us notice that, when this $input$ value has been determined, no simulator had terminated its associated e_sim_snapshot(). (If this was not the case, that simulator would have provided the other simulators with its own $input$ value.) Because processes are simulated deterministically, the *input* value returned contains the last value written by p_j as seen by q_i. This shows that the simulated process order is respected.

To ensure that the simulation is correct, we then have to show that the writes and snapshots of all processes can be linearized. The linearization point of the writes is placed at line 3 of Figure 4.2 of the first simulator that executes it. The linearization point of the snapshots is placed at line 01 of Figure 4.5 of the simulator q_i that imposes its *input_i* value.

Because the simulator q_i that imposes its *input_i* value in a e_sim_snapshot() operation reads the most advanced values at the time of its snapshot (lines 02–03 of Figure 4.5), and because once a simulator finishes the execution of e_sim_snapshot(), the value for this e_sim_snapshot() cannot change (Lemma 4.11), the linearization correspond to a linearization of a correct execution of the simulated algorithm. $\Box$*Lemma* 4.13

Theorem 4.14 *Algorithms* 4.2 *and* 4.5 *implement the colored BG simulation.*

Proof The proof follows from the Lemmas 4.9, 4.10, 4.12, and 4.13. $\Box$*Theorem* 4.14

4.7 CONCLUSION

This chapter presented the BG simulation, a powerful conceptual tool that allows a read/write system of n asynchronous processes that solve a distributed task despite the crash of up to $t = n - 1$ crashes to simulate a system of $m \geq n = t + 1$ asynchronous processes that solve the same task despite the crash of up to t processes.

More developments on the BG simulation are presented in [89]. The BG simulation has been extended to asynchronous message-passing systems prone to up to $t < n/3$ Byzantine processes in [45, 83].

CHAPTER 5

Anonymity

This chapter is an introduction to anonymity in systems where asynchronous crash-prone processes communicate through read/write registers. It considers three types of anonymity: process anonymity, memory anonymity, and full anonymity. In each case the chapter presents algorithms that solve classical distributed computing problems.

5.1 PROCESS ANONYMITY

5.1.1 DEFINITION OF PROCESS ANONYMITY

In a process anonymous computation model, it is not possible to distinguish the computing entities. So, the processes have no name, have the same code and the same local variables initialized to the same values.

Pioneering work on process-anonymity concerned message-passing systems [9] from which is extracted the following sentence:

"How much does each processor in a network of processors need to know about its own identity, the identities of other processors, and the underlying connection network in order for the network to be able to carry out useful functions?"

Early work on process anonymity in shared memory asynchronous systems appeared in [13]. Process anonymity is motivated by privacy requirements or by application specific requirements (e.g., sensors networks are made up of tiny entities that have no identifiers).

Notation The system model $CARW_{n,t}[\emptyset]$ with process anonymity is denoted $Pa\text{-}CARW_{n,t}[\emptyset]$. Moreover, at the presentation level an index is associated with each process, such that, if $i \neq j$, p_i and p_j are two different processes. Differently from the model $CARW_{n,t}[\emptyset]$ is that no process knows these indexes.

5.1.2 PROCESS-ANONYMOUS NON-BLOCKING MWMR SNAPSHOT

MWMR Snapshot object: definition Considering the model $Pa\text{-}CARW_{n,t}[t < n]$, a MWMR snapshot object $SNAP$ is an array of m MWMR (multi-writer multi-reader) atomic registers, that can be accessed only by the following two operations[1] denoted $SNAP[x].\text{write}()$ and $SNAP.\text{snapshot}()$. It is defined by the following properties.

---

[1] This snapshot object slightly differs from the one used in Chapter 4, which was an SWMR snapshot object. Let us notice that the notion of an SWMR object has no meaning in a process anonymous system: assigning specific registers to a process would conflict with process anonymity.

- The invocation of $SNAP[x].write(v)$ in $SNAP[x]$.

- The invocation of $SNAP[x].snapshot()$ returns the whole array $SNAP[1..m]$.

The two previous operations are atomic, which means that they appear as being executed instantaneously at different points of the time line of an omniscient external observer in such a way that, if op1 is terminated before op2 starts, op1 appears before op2. The resulting sequence of operations is called a linearization of the snapshot object, and we say that the operations are linearized.

Distributed algorithms implementing an MWMR snapshot memory in the non-anonymous system model $\mathcal{CARW}_{n,t}[t < n]$ (i.e., in the presence of any number of process crashes) are described in [82, 86].

Internal representation of the MWMR snapshot object At the implementation level, the snapshot object is represented by an array $SM[1..m]$ of m MWMR atomic read/write registers. Each register is initialized to the pair $\langle -, \perp \rangle$ (where $\perp$ is a default initial value). Hence, a register $SM[x]$ is a pair $SM[x] = \langle SM[x].ts, SM[x].value \rangle$ (such that only $SM[i].value$ can be made visible outside).

Each anonymous process p_i manages a local counter variable ts_i, initialized to 0, that it uses to associate a sequence number to its successive write operations into any atomic register $SM[x]$. Let us notice that two processes can associate the same sequence number to different write operations. A process p_i manages also three auxiliary variables denoted $count_i$, $sm1_i[1..m]$, and $sm2_i[1..m]$.

A non-blocking process-anonymous MWMR snapshot Algorithm 5.1 (due to R. Gurerraoui and E. Ruppert [63]) implements such an object. Let us remember that non-blocking is a progress condition stating that if processes invoke concurrently snapshot() and at least one of them does not crash, at least one of them terminates its invocation.

The operation write(), is self-explanatory. When a process p_i invokes snapshot(), it repeatedly (and asynchronously) reads the array $SM[1..m]$ until it obtains an array value $sm[1..m]$ that does not change during $(m(n - 1) + 2)$ consecutive readings of $SM[1..m]$. When this occurs, the invoking process returns the corresponding array value $sm[1..m]$.

Trivially, any write operation terminates (it the invoking process does not crash during the invocation). As far the snapshot operation is concerned, it is easy to see that, if there is a time after which a process (that does not crash) executes alone it terminates its snapshot operation, hence, the implementation is obstruction-free.

Assuming now that each process repeatedly invokes first $SNAP.write(x, v)$ (whatever x and v) followed by $SNAP.snapshot()$ (as done in nearly all uses of a snapshot object), let us show that the operation $SNAP.snapshot()$ is non-blocking. To this end, let us first observe that an invocation of $SNAP.snapshot()$ can be prevented from terminating only if processes issue permanently invocations of write(). The proof is by contradiction. Let us assume that no invocation of $SNAP.snapshot()$ terminates. This means that there are processes that permanently issue

---

Algorithm 5.1 Non-blocking snapshot object in $\mathcal{P}a\text{-}\mathcal{CARW}_{n,t}[t < n]$

```
operation write(x, v) is                                    % code for pᵢ
(1)      SM[x] ← ⟨tsᵢ, v⟩;
(2)      tsᵢ ← tsᵢ + 1;
(3)      return()
end of operation.

operation snapshot() is
(4)      countᵢ ← 1;
(5)      for each x ∈ {1, ..., m} do sm1ᵢ[x] ← SM[x] end for;
(6)      repeat forever
(7)          for each y ∈ {1, ..., m} do sm2ᵢ[y] ← SM[y] end for;
(8)          if (∀ x ∈ {1, ..., m} : sm1ᵢ[x] = sm2ᵢ[x])
(9)              then countᵢ ← countᵢ + 1;
(10)                  if (countᵢ = m(n − 1) + 2) then return(sm1ᵢ[1..m].value) end if
(11)              else countᵢ ← 1
(12)          end if;
(13)          sm1ᵢ[1..m] ← sm2ᵢ[1..m]
(14)      end repeat
enf of operation.
```

---

write operations. But this contradicts the assumption that each process alternates invocations of $SNAP[x]$.write() (whatever x) and REG.snapshot(). This is because, between two writes issued by a same process, this process invoked $SNAP$.snapshot(), and consequently this snapshot invocation terminated, which proves the non-blocking progress condition.

As far the linearization of the operations write() and snapshot() invoked by the processes is concerned we have the following. Let us consider an invocation of snapshot() that terminates. It has seen $m(n − 1) + 2$ times the same vector $sm[1..m]$ in the array $SM[1..m]$. Since a given pair $⟨ts, v⟩$ can be written at most once by a process, it can be written at most $(n − 1)$ times during a snapshot() (once by each process, except the one invoking the snapshot). It follows that, among the $m(n − 1) + 2$ times where the same vector $sm[1..m]$ was read from $SM[1..m]$, there are least two consecutive reads during which no process wrote a register. The snapshot invocation is consequently linearized between these two sequential reads on the array $SM[1..m]$.

Remark The interested reader will find in [63] a (more intricate) algorithm implementing a wait-free process-anonymous snapshot object. It follows that, as far progress conditions are concerned, process-anonymity does create a computability threshold for snapshot objects.

5.1.3 PROCESS-ANONYMOUS OBSTRUCTION-FREE BINARY CONSENSUS

In the binary consensus problem, a process can propose only 0 or 1. As seen in Chapter 1, it is impossible to implement a consensus object satisfying the wait-freedom progress condition in the model $\mathcal{CARW}_{n,t}[t < n]$. So it is impossible also in the model $\mathcal{P}a\text{-}\mathcal{CARW}_{n,t}[t < n]$.

This section presents an obstruction-free binary consensus algorithm for the system model $Pa\text{-}CARW_{n,t}[t < n]$. Let us remember that "obstruction-freedom" means that if a process executes alone for a long enough period of time (and does not crash) it terminates its operation. Algorithm 5.2 presents such an algorithm (introduced in [63]).

Internal representation of the binary consensus object   At the implementation level, the consensus object is represented by a two-dimensional array $SM[0, \ldots, 1, 1 \ldots]$ (whose second dimension is unbounded) of MWMR atomic read/write registers. Each entry $SM[x, y]$ is initialized to the default value down and can later take the value up. $SM[x, y]$ can be seen as flag which is raised by a process (and remains then raised forever) when some condition is satisfied.

A process p_i locally manages a current estimate of the decision value est_i, an iteration number k_i and an auxiliary variable $opposite_i$.

Algorithm 5.2 Obstruction-free binary consensus object in $Pa\text{-}CARW_{n,t}[t < n]$

```
operation propose(vᵢ) is                                          % code for pᵢ
(1)     estᵢ ← v; kᵢ ← 0;
(2)     repeat forever
(3)         kᵢ ← kᵢ + 1; let oppositeᵢ = 1 − estᵢ;
(4)         if (SM[oppositeᵢ, kᵢ] = down)
(5)             then SM[estᵢ, kᵢ] ← up;
(6)                 if (kᵢ > 1) ∧ (SM[oppositeᵢ, kᵢ − 1] = down) then return(estᵢ) end if
(7)             else estᵢ ← oppositeᵢ
(8)         end if
(9)     end repeat
end of operation.
```

Description of the algorithm   To understand the behavior of the algorithm, the reader is encouraged to execute it first when a single value is proposed, and then when both values are proposed. The algorithm can be seen as ruling a competition between two teams of processes, the team of the processes that champion 0, and the team of the processes that champion 1.

A process p_i first progresses to its next iteration (line 3). Iteration numbers k can be seen as defining a sequence of rounds executed asynchronously by the processes. Hence, the state of the flags $SM[0, k]$ and $SM[1, k]$ (which are up or down) describes the state of the competition at round k. When a process p_i enters round k, there are two cases.

- If the flag associated with this round and the other value is up ($SM[opposite_i, k] =$ up, i.e., the predicate of line 4 is not satisfied), p_i changes its mind passing from the group of processes that champion est_i to the group of processes that champion $opposite_i$ (line 7). It then proceeds to the next round.

- If the flag associated with this round and the other value is down (the predicate of line 4 is then satisfied), maybe est_i can be decided. To this end, p_i indicates first that est_i is competing to be the decided value by raising the round k flag $SM[est_i, k]$ (line 5). The decision involves the two last rounds, namely $(k-1)$ and k, attained by p_i (hence, the sub-predicate $k > 1$ at line 6). If p_i sees both the flags measuring the progress of $\overline{est_i}$ equal to down at round $(k-1)$ and round k (predicate $SM[opposite_i, k]$ at line 4, and predicate $SM[opposite_i, k]$ at line 6), $opposite_i$ is defeated, and p_i consequently decides est_i.

To show this is correct, let us consider the smallest round k during which a process decides. Moreover, let p_i be a process that decides during this round, v the value it decides, and τ the time at which p_i reads $SM[\overline{v}, k-1]$ before deciding (line 6 of round k). As p_i decides, at time τ we have $SM[\overline{v}, k-1] = $ down. This means that, before time τ, no process changed its mind from v to $\overline{v}$ at line 6. The rest of the proof consists in showing that no process p_j started round k before time τ with $est_j = \overline{v}$. A full proof of this algorithm ensures the consensus is given in [63].

5.1.4 ON THE COMPUTABILITY SIDE

The three following computability-related results (stated and proved in [25]) are associated with the $\mathcal{P}a\text{-}\mathcal{CARW}_{n,t}[t < n]$ model (tasks are defined in Chapter 4).

- Let O be an object that can be obstruction-free implemented in $\mathcal{P}a\text{-}\mathcal{CARW}_{n,t}[t < n]$ with any number of atomic registers. O can be obstruction-free implemented in $\mathcal{P}a\text{-}\mathcal{CARW}_{n,t}[t < n]$ with n MWMR atomic read/write registers.

- If a task $T = (\Delta, \mathcal{I}, \mathcal{O})$ is obstruction-free solvable in $\mathcal{P}a\text{-}\mathcal{CARW}_{n,t}[t < n]$ (with any number of MWMR atomic read/write registers), then it can be obstruction-free solvable in $\mathcal{P}a\text{-}\mathcal{CARW}_{n,t}[t < n]$ with no more than n MWMR atomic read/write registers.

- If a colorless task $T = (\Delta, \mathcal{I}, \mathcal{O})$ is obstruction-free solvable in $\mathcal{CARW}_{n,t}[t < n]$ with any number of single-writer/multi-reader (SWMR) registers, it is also obstruction-free solvable in $\mathcal{P}a\text{-}\mathcal{CARW}_{n,t}[t < n]$ with n MWMR atomic registers.

5.2 MEMORY ANONYMITY

5.2.1 DEFINITION OF MEMORY ANONYMITY

The notion of memory anonymity has been implicitly used in some works since the 1980s (e.g., [111]), but it has been explicitly defined and investigated as a concept by G. Taubenfeld in [135]. More precisely, this paper considers the case where "there is no *a priori* agreement between processes on the names of shared memory locations." Considering a shared memory defined as an array $SM[1..m]$ of memory locations (registers) memory anonymity means that, while the same location identifier $SM[x]$ always denotes the same memory location for a process

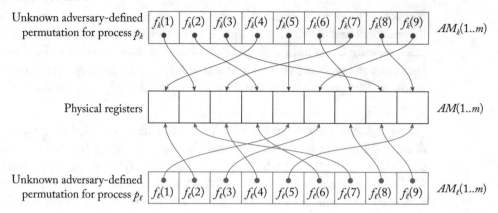

Figure 5.1: Example of an anonymous memory.

p_i, it does not necessarily denote the same memory location for two different processes p_i and p_j.

Definition More formally, an anonymous memory $AM[1..m]$ is defined as follows:

- for each process p_i an adversary defined a permutation $f_i()$ over the set $\{1, 2, \ldots, m\}$, such that when p_i uses the address $AM[x]$, it actually accesses $AM[f_i(x)]$,

- no process knows the permutations, and

- all the registers are initialized to the same default value denoted $\perp$.

An example of anonymous memory is described in Figure 5.1.

Notation The asynchronous system model $\mathcal{CARW}_{n,t}[\emptyset]$, where all the m atomic read/write registers are anonymous, is denoted $\mathcal{Ma\text{-}CARW}_{n,t,m}[\emptyset]$.

Given a process p_i, the notation $AM_i[x]$ is used to denote the register of the shared anonymous memory with index x used by p_i. This makes more apparent the fact that $AM_i[x]$ and $AM_j[x]$ can denote different registers.

5.2.2 MEMORY-ANONYMOUS OBSTRUCTION-FREE MULTIVALUED CONSENSUS

This section presents Algorithm 5.3 which implements an obstruction-free multivalued consensus object in the model $\mathcal{Ma\text{-}CARW}_{n,t,m}[m = 2n - 1]$. The algorithm is due to G. Taubenfeld [135].

Internal representation of the consensus object The consensus object is represented by an array $AM[1..2n - 1]$ of atomic read/write registers. Each $AM[x]$ is composed of two fields:

$AM[x].id$ which contains a process identity, and $SM[x].val$ which contains a value proposed by a process. Each $AM[x]$ is initialized to $\langle -, \perp \rangle$.

Local variables at a process p_i Each process p_i manages three local variables. One is an array $sm_i[1..2n - 1]$ (in which p_i saves its reading of $AM_i[1..2n - 1]$). The variable est_i contains the current estimate of the decision value, as known by p_i. Finally, k_i is a local index.

Algorithm   When a process p_i invokes propose(v_i), where v_i is the value it proposes, it first assigns v_i to est_i (line 1). Then p_i enters a loop, in which it first reads asynchronously the shared anonymous memory $AM_i[1..2n - 1]$ (line 3). If it sees a majority value v (line 4), p_i adopts it as new estimate (line 5).

Algorithm 5.3 Obstruction-free multivalued consensus in $\mathcal{M}a\text{-}\mathcal{CARW}_{n,t,m}[t < n, m = 2n - 1]$

```
operation propose(vᵢ) is                          % code for pᵢ
(1)     estᵢ ← v;
(2)     repeat
(3)         for each kᵢ ∈ {1,...,2n − 1} do smᵢ[kᵢ] ← AMᵢ[kᵢ] end for;
(4)         if (∃v ≠ ⊥ : |{k such that smᵢ[k].val = v}| ≥ n)
(5)             then estᵢ ← v
(6)         end if;
(7)         if (∃ x ∈ {1,...,2n − 1} such that smᵢ[x] ≠ ⟨i, estᵢ⟩)
(8)             then SMᵢ[x] ← ⟨i, estᵢ⟩
(9)         end if
(10)        until smᵢ[1..2n − 1] = [⟨i, estᵢ⟩,...,⟨i, estᵢ⟩] end repeat;
(11)        return(estᵢ)
end of operation.
```

Then, if it sees an entry $sm_i[x]$ that does not contain the pair $\langle i, est_i \rangle$, p_i writes this pair in $SM_i[x]$ (lines 7–8). Finally, if all entries of $sm_i[1..2n - 1]$ contain the pair $\langle i, est_i \rangle$, p_i decides the value saved in est_i (predicate of lines 10 and 11), otherwise it re-enters the loop.

Sketch of proof   Let us first consider the agreement property. Let p_i be the first process that decides, and let v be the value it decides. It follows from line 10 that, before deciding, p_i was such that $sm_i[1..2n - 1] = [\langle i, est_i \rangle, \ldots, \langle i, est_i \rangle]$, i.e., p_i has seen all entries of $AM[1..2n - 1]$ equal to $\langle i, est_i \rangle$. Each other process p_j may write into one of the shared registers at line 8, overwriting the pair $\langle i, est_i \rangle$. It follows that at most $(n - 1)$ entries of $AM[1..2n - 1]$ can be overwritten to a value different from $\langle i, est_i \rangle$. Consequently, when, after it read the shared array $AM[1..2n - 1]$ at line 3, any other process p_j will find that v satisfies the predicate of line 4, and consequently will adopt v as new estimate (line 4). If follows that no value different from v can be decided.

To prove that the implementation is obstruction-free, let us consider that after some time only one process p_i progresses and does not crash. Hence, all the other processes stop executing their code at any line of the algorithm. It is easy to see that, after some finite time, p_i will have written the same estimate value v in all the anonymous registers. When this occurs, p_i decides the estimate value v.

A more general obstruction-free algorithm solving k-set agreement with only $(n - k + 1)$ MWMR atomic read/write registers is described in [25].

5.3 FULL ANONYMITY

Definition   In a fully anonymous system both the processes and the memory are anonymous. Such a system is denoted $\mathcal{F}a\text{-}\mathcal{CARW}_{n,t,m}[\emptyset]$.

5.3.1 SET-AGREEMENT OBJECT

Such an object is in some sense dual of consensus: each process is assumed to propose a value, and if all the values are different, one of them must be eliminated. Hence, as consensus, a set-agreement is defined by a single operation denoted **propose()**, that proposes a value and returns a value. The following three properties defines set-agreement.

- Validity. If a process decides a value, that value has been proposed by a process.

- At most, $(n - 1)$ different values are decided.

- Termination. If a process executes alone during a long enough period of time it decides a value.

5.3.2 OBSTRUCTION-FREE SET-AGREEMENT DESPITE FULL ANONYMITY

This section presents Algorithm 5.4 (due to M. Raynal and G. Taubenfeld [125]) which is a fully anonymous obstruction-free set-agreement algorithm.

The shared memory is composed of $m \geq 3$ anonymous read/write atomic registers, so the system model is $\mathcal{F}a\text{-}\mathcal{CARW}_{n,t,m}[m > 3]$. Let $AM[1..m]$ denote the shared memory. Each process p_i has two local variables $am_i[1..m]$ where it store its last local copy of $AM[1..m]$, and a variable est_i where it stores its local estimate of the value it will decide.

When it invokes **propose**(v), the process p_i first saves v in its local variable est_i (line 1). Then it asynchronously scans the anonymous memory (line 3), and update its local estimate if there is a majority value (lines 4–6). Then p_i searches if there an entry of the memory that does not contain its estimate (line 7). If it is the case, it write its estimate value in this entry of the shared memory (line 8). This is repeated until all the registers of the anonymous memory contain the value of est_i (line 9). When this occurs, p_i decides the value if est_i (line 10). A proof of this algorithm can be found in [125].

Algorithm 5.4 Obstruction-free set-agreement in $\mathcal{F}a\text{-}\mathcal{CARW}_{n,t,m}[n > t, m \geq 3]$

```
operation propose(v) is                                    % code for p_i
(1)      est_i ← v;
(2)      repeat
(3)         for each k ∈ {1,...,m} do am_i[k] ← AM_i[k] end for;
(4)         if (∃ w ≠ ⊥ which appears in more than m/2 entries of am_i[1..m]
(5)            then est_i ← w
(6)         end if;
(7)         if (∃ k such that am_i[k] ≠ est_i) then j ← k else j ← ⊥ end if;
(8)         if (j ≠ ⊥) then AM_i[j] ← est_i end if;
(9)         until (∀ j ∈ {1,...,m}: am_i[k] = est_i end repeat;
(10)     return(est_i)
end of operation.
```

5.3.3 FULLY ANONYMOUS CONSENSUS IN $\mathcal{F}a\text{-}\mathcal{CARW}_{n,t,m}[t < n, \textbf{Compare\&Swap}]$

As seen in Chapters 1 and 2, one way to cope with the impossibility to build a wait-free consensus object in the presence of asynchrony and process crashes consists in enriching the system model with an operation whose consensus number is $+\infty$.

The same holds when, in addition, the system is fully anonymous. So let us enrich the system model $\mathcal{F}a\text{-}\mathcal{CARW}_{n,t,m}[\emptyset]$ with the atomic operation Compare&swap(), which provides us with the model $\mathcal{F}a\text{-}\mathcal{CARW}_{n,t,m}[\text{Compare\&swap}]$. The shared anonymous memory $AM[1..m]$, where $m \geq 1$, is initialized to $[\bot, \ldots, \bot]$. Each anonymous process p_i manages two local variables est_i and $am_i[1..m]$.

Considering such a model, Algorithm 5.5 presents a multivalued consensus object (due to [125]).

Algorithm 5.5 Wait-free consensus in $\mathcal{F}a\text{-}\mathcal{CARW}_{n,t,m}[t < n, \text{Compare\&Swap}]$

```
operation propose(v) is
(1)      for each k ∈ {1,...,m} do AM_i[k].Compare&swap(⊥, v) end for;
(2)      for each k ∈ {1,...,m} do am_i[k] ← AM_i[k] end for;
(3)      est_i ← max(am_i[1],...,am_i[m]);
(4)      return(est_i)
end of operation.
```

It is assumed that the proposed values are totally ordered and that $\bot$ is smaller than any of them. When p_i invokes propose(v) it scans the anonymous memory with the operation Compare&swap(), and atomically writes the value v it proposes, in each register containing $\bot$. Then p_i reads the whole anonymous memory and computes the maximal value it contains, which is returned as the decided value.

Let us observe that after a process has executed line 1, no anonymous register contains the value $\perp$. So, assuming that at least one process does not crash, there a time after which (whatever the asynchrony/crash pattern) all the registers of the anonymous memory contains a non-$\perp$ value. As the processes apply the same deterministic rule to extract a value from the values deposited in $AM[1..m]$, they decide the same value.

5.4 CONCLUSION

This chapter presented algorithms solving agreement problems in a context where, in addition to the traditional adversaries that are asynchrony and process crashes, algorithms have to cope with anonymous processes and/or anonymous memory.

5.5 APPENDIX: THE CASE OF RELIABLE FULLY ANONYMOUS SYSTEMS

This section considers reliable fully anonymous systems, i.e., system model $\mathcal{F}a\text{-}\mathcal{CARW}_{n,t,m}[t = 0]$. In this context it addresses two problems which cannot be solved in the presence of failures, namely mutual exclusion and leader election.

5.5.1 DEADLOCK-FREE MUTUAL EXCLUSION IN $\mathcal{F}a\text{-}\mathcal{CARW}_{n,t,m}[t = 0]$

Definition Mutual exclusion (in short mutex), introduced in the 1960s by E. W. Dijkstra [43], is the first cooperation problem that has been stated and solved. It consists in building a lock object providing the processes with the operations acquire() and release(). These operations are used to bracket some part of code (known under the name *critical section*) as follows:

$$\text{acquire();} \quad \textit{critical section;} \quad \text{release(),}$$

in such a way that no two processes can execute simultaneously the code defining the critical section. Assuming that the code of the critical section terminates, mutual exclusion is defined by the following properties.

- Mutual exclusion (safety). No two processes can be simultaneously in the critical section.

- Deadlock-freedom (liveness). If there is a process p_i that has a pending operation acquire() (i.e., it invoked acquire() and its invocation is not terminated) and there is no process inside the critical section, then some process p_j (possibly $p_j \neq p_i$) eventually enters the critical section(i.e., returns from its invocation of acquire().

Results Let $M(n)$ be the set of all the integers that are relatively prime with all the integers smaller or equal to n:

$$M(n) = \{m \text{ such that } \forall \ell \in \{1,\dots,n\} \; : \; \gcd(\ell,m) = 1\}.$$

In [126] the authors (i) show that there is no mutex algorithm in the model $\mathcal{F}a\text{-}\mathcal{C}ARW_{n,tm}[t=0]$, (ii) present a mutex algorithm for the model $\mathcal{F}a\text{-}\mathcal{C}ARW_{n,tm}[t=0, \mathsf{Compare\&swap}, m \in M(n)]$, and (iii) prove that the condition $m \in M(n)$ is necessary to solve mutex on top of a fully anonymous system. This means that $m \in M(n)$ is the minimal asymmetry seed needed to solve mutex despite the net effect of asynchrony and full anonymity.

5.5.2   ELECTION IN $\mathcal{F}a\text{-}\mathcal{C}ARW_{n,t,m}[t=0]$

Definition   In a process anonymous system made up of n processes election consists in providing each process p_i with a local Boolean variable $elected_i$, which, initialized to `false`, is set to `true` if and only if p_i is elected.

The election problem can be decomposed into two classes according to the constraint on the number of processes that can/must be elected. Let d be such that $1 \leq d < n$.

- d-Election requires that at least one and at most d processes are elected.

- Exact d-election requires that exactly d processes are elected.

Moreover, an election algorithm may require or not the participation of all the processes.

Results   Let $M(n, d) = \{k$ such that $\forall \ell \in \{1, \ldots, n\} : \mathsf{gcd}(\ell, k) \leq d\}$. The following results are presented in [85] for the system model $\mathcal{F}a\text{-}\mathcal{C}ARW_{n,t,m}[t=0, \mathsf{Compare\&swap}]$.

- d-Election when participation is not required is possible if and only if $m \in M(n, d)$.

- Exact d-election with required participation is possible if and only if $\mathsf{gcd}(m, n)$ divides d.

- d-Election with required participation is possible if and only if $\mathsf{gcd}(m, n) \leq d$.

- Both problems cannot be solved when communication through only read-write registers.

Bibliography

[1] Afek Y., Attiya H., Dolev D., Gafni E., Merritt M., and Shavit N., Atomic snapshots of shared memory. *Journal of the ACM*, 40(4):873–890, 1993. DOI: 10.1145/153724.153741 44, 54, 58, 73

[2] Afek Y., Dauber D., and Touitou D., Wait-free made fast. *Proc. 27th ACM Symposium on Theory of Computing (STOC'95)*, pages 538–547, ACM Press, 1995. DOI: 10.1145/225058.225271 17, 18

[3] Afek Y., Ellen F., and Gafni E., Deterministic objects: Life beyond consensus. *Proc. 35th ACM Symposium on Principles of Distributed Computing (PODC'16)*, pages 97–106, ACM Press, 2016. DOI: 10.1145/2933057.2933116 36, 47, 49, 50

[4] Afek Y., Gafni E., Rajsbaum S., Raynal M., and Travers C., The k-simultaneous consensus problem. *Distributed Computing*, 22(3):185–195, 2010. DOI: 10.1007/s00446-009-0090-8 25, 26, 72

[5] Akl S. G., *The Design and Analysis of Parallel Algorithms*. Prentice Hall International Series, 401 pages, 1989. 53

[6] Aguilera M. K., Frolund S., Hadzilacos V., Horn S. L., and Toueg S., Abortable and query-abortable objects and their efficient implementation. *Proc. 26th ACM Symposium on Principles of Distributed Computing (PODC'07)*, pages 23–32, ACM Press, 2007. DOI: 10.1145/1281100.1281107 19

[7] Anderson J. H., Multi-writer composite registers. *Distributed Computing*, 7(4):175–195, 1994. DOI: 10.1007/bf02280833 73

[8] Anderson J. and Moir M., Universal constructions for large objects. *IEEE Transactions on Parallel and Distributed Systems*, 10(12):1317–1332, 1999. DOI: 10.1109/71.819952 17, 18, 21

[9] Anguin D., Local and global properties in networks of processes. *Proc. 12th Symposium on Theory of Computing (STOC'80)*, pages 82–93, ACM Press, 1980. DOI: 10.1145/800141.804655 87

[10] Attiya H., Bar-Noy A., Dolev D., Peleg D., and Reischuk R., Renaming in an asynchronous environment. *Journal of the ACM*, 37(3):524–548, 1990. DOI: 10.1145/79147.79158 54, 58, 72, 73

[11] Attiya H. and Ellen F., *Impossibility Results for Distributed Computing*. Synthesis Lectures on Distributed Computing Theory, Morgan & Claypool Publishers, 162 pages, 2014. xxi

[12] Attiya H., Fouren A., and Gafni E., An adaptive collect algorithm with applications. *Distributed Computing*, 15(2):87–96, 2002. DOI: 10.1007/s004460100067 54

[13] Attiya H., Gorbach A., and Moran S., Computing in totally anonymous asynchronous shared-memory systems. *Information and Computation*, 173(2):162–183, 2002. DOI: 10.1006/inco.2001.3119 87

[14] Attiya H., Herlihy M., and Rachman O., Atomic snapshots using lattice agreement. *Distributed Computing*, 8(3):121–132, 1995. DOI: 10.1007/bf02242714 54

[15] Attiya H. and Welch J. L., *Distributed Computing: Fundamentals, Simulations, and Advanced Topics*, 2nd ed., Wiley-Interscience, 414 pages, 2004. 54, 73

[16] Bar-Noy A., Dolev D., Dwork C., and Strong R., Shifting gears: Changing algorithms on the fly to expedite Byzantine agreement. *Information and Computation*, 97(2):205–233, 1992. DOI: 10.1016/0890-5401(92)90035-e 54

[17] Bartlett K. A., Scantlebury S. A., and Wilkinson P. T., A note on reliable full-duplex transmission over half-duplex links. *Communications of the ACM*, 12(5):260–261, 1969. DOI: 10.1145/362946.362970 13

[18] Bédin D., Lépine F., Mostéfaoui A., Perez D., and Perrin M., Compare-and-swap is not the most suitable special instruction for multi-threaded systems. *Unpublished Manuscript*, 12 pages, 2020. 14

[19] Bédin D., Lépine F., Mostéfaoui A., Perez D., and Perrin M., Wait-free CAS-based algorithms: The burden of the past. *Proc. 35th International Symposium on Distributed Computing (DISC'21)*, Volume abcd, 15 pages, LIPICs, 2021. 22

[20] Ben-David N., Cheng Chan D. Y., Hadzilacos V., and Toueg S., k-Abortable objects: Progress under high contention. *Proc. 30th International Symposium on Distributed Computing (DISC'16)*, pages 298–312, Springer LNCS 9888, 2016. DOI: 10.1007/978-3-662-53426-7_22 20

[21] Berryhill R., Golab W., and Tripunitara M., Robust shared objects for non-volatile main memory. *Proc. 19th International Conference on Principles of Distributed Systems (OPODIS'15)*, 46:20:1–20:17, LIPICs, 2015. 41

[22] Borowsky E. and Gafni E., Generalized FLP impossibility results for t-resilient asynchronous computations. *Proc. 25th ACM Symposium on Theory of Computing (STOC'93)*, pages 91–100, ACM Press, 1993. DOI: 10.1145/167088.167119 25, 37, 38, 43, 44, 46, 71, 72, 74, 76

[23] Borowsky E. and Gafni E., Immediate atomic snapshots and fast renaming. *Proc. 12th ACM Symposium on Principles of Distributed Computing (PODC'93)*, pages 41–51, 1993. DOI: 10.1145/164051.164056 45, 54, 58

[24] Borowsky E., Gafni E., Lynch N., and Rajsbaum S., The BG distributed simulation algorithm. *Distributed Computing*, 14(3):127–146, 2001. DOI: 10.1007/pl00008933 71, 72, 73, 75, 76

[25] Bouzid Z., Raynal M., and Sutra P., Anonymous obstruction-free (n, k)-set agreement with $(n - k + 1)$ atomic read/write registers. *Distributed Computing*, 31(2):99–117, 2018. DOI: 10.1007/s00446-017-0301-7 33, 91, 94

[26] Bouzid Z. and Travers C., Parallel consensus is harder than set agreement in message passing. *Proc. 33rd International IEEE Conference on Distributed Computing Systems (ICDCS'13)*, pages 611–620, IEEE Press, 2013. DOI: 10.1109/ICDCS.2013.72. 26

[27] Brinch Hansen, P., *The Origin of Concurrent Programming*. 534 pages, Springer, 2002. DOI: 10.1007/978-1-4757-3472-0 7

[28] Bushkov V. and Guerraoui G., Safety-liveness exclusion in distributed computing. *Proc. 34th ACM Symposium on Principles of Distributed Computing (PODC'15)*, pages 227–236, ACM Press, 2015. DOI: 10.1145/2767386.2767401 7

[29] Capdevielle C., Johnen C., and Milani A., Solo-fast universal constructions for deterministic abortable objects. *Proc. 28th International Symposium on Distributed Computing (DISC'14)*, pages 288–302, Springer LNCS 8784, 2014. DOI: 10.1007/978-3-662-45174-8_20 19, 20

[30] Castañeda A. and Rajsbaum S., New combinatorial topology bounds for renaming: The upper bound. *Journal of the ACM*, 59(1):3:1–3:49, 2012. DOI: 10.1145/2108242.2108245 72

[31] Castañeda A., Rajsbaum S., and Raynal M., The renaming problem in shared memory systems: An introduction. *Elsevier Computer Science Review*, 5:229–251, 2011. DOI: 10.1016/j.cosrev.2011.04.001 45, 58, 72

[32] Castañeda A., Rajsbaum S., and Raynal M., Unifying concurrent objects and distributed tasks: Interval-linearizability. *Journal of the ACM*, 65(6), 42 pages, 2018. DOI: 10.1145/3266457 57

[33] Censor-Hillel K., Petrank E., and Timnat S., Help! *Proc. 34th Symposium on Principles of Distributed Computing (PODC'15)*, pages 241–250, ACM Press, 2015. DOI: 10.1145/2767386.2767415 9, 36

[34] Chan D. Y. C., Hadzilacos V., and Toueg S., Life beyond set agreement. *Proc. 36th ACM Symposium on Principles of Distributed Computing (PODC'17)*, pages 345–354, ACM Press, 2017. DOI: 10.1145/3087801.3087822 41

[35] Chandra T. D. and Toueg S., Unreliable failure detectors for reliable distributed systems. *Journal of the ACM*, 43(2):225–267, 1996. DOI: 10.1145/226643.226647 23

[36] Chan D. Y. C., Hadzilacos V., and Toueg S., On the classification of deterministic objects via set agreement power. *Proc. 37th ACM Symposium on Principles of Distributed Computing (PODC'18)*, pages 71–80, ACM Press, 2018. DOI: 10.1145/3212734.3212775 41

[37] Chaudhuri S., More choices allow more faults: Set consensus problems in totally asynchronous systems. *Information and Computation*, 105(1):132–158, 1993. DOI: 10.1006/inco.1993.1043 25, 37

[38] Chaudhuri S. and Reiners P., Understanding the set consensus partial order using the Borowsky–Gafni simulation. *Proc. 10th International Workshop on Distributed Algorithms*, pages 362–379, Springer LNCS 1151, 1996. DOI: 10.1007/3-540-61769-8_23 41, 46, 47

[39] Crain T., Imbs D., and Raynal M., Towards a universal construction for transaction-based multiprocess programs. *Theoretical Computer Science*, 496:154–169, 2013. DOI: 10.1016/j.tcs.2012.09.011 33

[40] Daian E., Losa G., Afek Y., and Gafni E., A wealth of sub-consensus deterministic objects. *Proc. 32nd International Symposium on Distributed Computing (DISC'18)*, Article 17, 17 pages, LIPICS 121, 2018. DOI: 10.4230/LIPIcs.DISC.2018.17 36, 42, 44

[41] Dahl O. J., Dijkstra E. W., and Hoare C. A. R., *Structured Programming*. 220 pages, Academic Press, 1972. 53

[42] Delporte-Gallet C., Fauconnier H., Gafni E., and Kuznetsov P., Set consensus collections are decidable. *Proc. 20th International Conference on Principles of Distributed Computing (OPODIS'16)*, 70(7), 17 pages, LIPICS, 2016. 41

[43] Dijkstra E .W., Solution of a problem in concurrent programming control. *Communications of the ACM*, 8(9):569, 1965. DOI: 10.1145/365559.365617 78, 96

[44] Doherty S., Groves L., Luchangco V., and Moir M., Towards formally specifying and verifying transactional memory. *Formal Aspects of Computing*, 25:769–799, 2013. DOI: 10.1007/s00165-012-0225-8 33

[45] Dolev D. and Gafni E., Some garbage in—some garbage out: Asynchronous t-Byzantine as asynchronous benign t-resilient system with fixed t-Trojan-horse inputs. *CoRR*, 2016. 86

[46] Ellen F., Fatourou P., Kosmas E., Milani A., and Travers C., Universal constructions that ensure disjoint-access parallelism and wait-freedom. *Distributed Computing*, 29:251–277, 2016. DOI: 10.1007/s00446-015-0261-8 18

[47] Ellen F., Gelashvili G., Shavit N., and Zhu L., A complexity-based hierarchy for multiprocessor synchronization. *Distributed Computing*, 33(2):125–144, 2020. DOI: 10.1145/2933057.2933113 21, 38, 39

[48] Fatourou P. and Kallimanis N. D., The RedBlue adaptive universal constructions. *Proc. 23rd Symposium on Distributed Computing (DISC'09)*, pages 127–141, Springer LNCS 5805, 2009. DOI: 10.1007/978-3-642-04355-0_15 9, 18

[49] Fatourou P. and Kallimanis N. D., Highly-efficient wait-free synchronization. *Theory of Computing Systems*, 55:475–520, 2014. DOI: 10.1007/s00224-013-9491-y 10

[50] Fischer M. J., Lynch N. A., and Paterson M. S., Impossibility of distributed consensus with one faulty process. *Journal of the ACM*, 32(2):374–382, 1985. DOI: 10.1145/3149.214121 4, 8, 35, 56, 73

[51] Francez N., Hailpern B., and Taubendfeld G., Script: A communication abstraction mechanism and its verification. *Science of Computer Programming*, 6:35–88, 1986. DOI: 10.1016/0167-6423(86)90018-3 54

[52] Gafni E., Round-by-round fault detectors: Unifying synchrony and asynchrony. *Proc. 17th ACM Symposium on Principles of Distributed Computing (PODC)*, pages 143–152, ACM Press, 1998. 26, 27

[53] Gafni E., The extended BG simulation and the characterization of t-tesiliency. *Proc. 41th ACM Symposium on Theory of Computing (STOC'09)*, pages 85–92, ACM Press, 2009. DOI: 10.1145/1536414.1536428 72

[54] Gafni E. and Guerraoui R., Generalizing universality. *Proc. 22nd International Conference on Concurrency Theory (CONCUR'11)*, pages 17–27, Springer LNCS 6901, 2011. 26, 29

[55] Gafni E. and Kuznetsov P., On set consensus numbers. *Distributed Computing*, 23(3–4):149–163, 2011. DOI: 10.1007/s00446-011-0142-8 41

[56] Gafni E., Mostéfaoui, Raynal M., and Travers C., From adaptive renaming to set agreement. *Theoretical Computer Science*, 410(14–15):1328–1335, 2009. DOI: 10.1016/j.tcs.2008.05.016 44, 47

[57] Gafni E. and Rajsbaum S., Recursion in distributed computing. *Proc. 12th International Symposium on Stabilization, Safety, and Security of Distributed Systems (SSS'10)*, pages 362–376, Springer LNCS 6366, 2010. DOI: 10.1007/978-3-642-16023-3_30 54, 61, 64

[58] Gafni E., Raynal M., and Travers C., Test&set, adaptive renaming and set agreement: A guided visit to asynchronous computability. *Proc. 26th IEEE Symposium on Reliable Distributed Systems (SRDS'07)*, pages 93–102, IEEE Computer Society Press, 2007. DOI: 10.1109/SRDS.2007.8 39

[59] Golab W., The recoverable consensus hierarchy (brief announcement). *Proc. 38th ACM Symposium on Principles of Distributed Computing (PODC'19)*, pages 212–215, ACM Press, 2019. Full version: Recoverable consensus in shared memory, *ArXiv:1804.10597v2*, 2018. 41, 42

[60] Gray J., Notes on database operating systems. *Advanced Course on Operating Systems*, pages 393–481, Springer LNCS 60, 1978. DOI: 10.1007/3-540-08755-9_9 19, 32

[61] Guerraoui R. and Kapalka M., On the correctness of transactional memory. *Proc. 3rd ACM Symposium on Principles an Practice of Parallel Programming (PPOPP'03)*, pages 175–184, ACM Press, 2008. DOI: 10.1145/1345206.1345233 33

[62] Guerraoui R. and Raynal M., A universal construction for wait-free objects. *Proc. Workshop on Foundations of Fault-Tolerant Distributed Computing (FOFDC)*, pages 959–966, Computer Society Press, 2007. 23

[63] Guerraoui R. and Ruppert E., Anonymous and fault-tolerant shared-memory computations. *Distributed Computing*, 20:165–177, 2007. DOI: 10.1007/s00446-007-0042-0 88, 89, 90, 91

[64] Hadzilacos V. and Toueg S., On deterministic abortable objects. *Proc. 35th ACM symposium on Principles of Distributed Computing (PODC'13)*, pages 4–12, ACM Press, 2013. DOI: 10.1145/2484239.2484241 19

[65] Harel D. and Feldman Y., *Algorithmics: The Spirit of Computing*, 3rd ed., 572 pages, Springer, 2012. xxi, 4, 53

[66] Herlihy M. P., Wait-free synchronization. *ACM Transactions on Programming Languages and Systems*, 13(1):124–149, 1991. DOI: 10.1145/114005.102808 4, 7, 8, 9, 25, 35, 36, 37, 40, 56

[67] Herlihy M. P., A methodology for implementing highly concurrent data objects. *ACM Transactions on Programming Languages and Systems*, 15(5):745–770, 1993. DOI: 10.1145/161468.161469 9, 17, 18

[68] Herlihy M. P., Kozlov D., and Rajsbaum S., *Distributed Computing Through Combinatorial Topology*, 336 pages, Morgan Kaufmann/Elsevier, 2014. 72

[69] Herlihy M. P., Luchangco V., and Moir M., Obstruction-free synchronization: Double-ended queues as an example. *Proc. 23th International IEEE Conference on Distributed Computing Systems (ICDCS'03)*, pages 522–529, IEEE Press, 2003. DOI: 10.1109/icdcs.2003.1203503 7, 40

[70] Herlihy M. and Moss J. E. B., Transactional memory: Architectural support for lock-free data structures. *Proc. 20th Annual International Symposium on Computer Architecture (ISCA'93)*, pages 289–300, ACM Press, 1993. DOI: 10.1145/173682.165164 32

[71] Herlihy M. P. and Rajsbaum R., Algebraic spans. *Mathematical Structures in Computer Science*, 10(4):549–573, 2000. DOI: 10.1017/s0960129500003170 46, 47

[72] Herlihy M., Rajsbaum S., and Raynal M., Power and limits of distributed computing shared memory models. *Theoretical Computer Science*, 509:3–24, 2013. DOI: 10.1016/j.tcs.2013.03.002 4, 57, 72

[73] Herlihy M., Rajsbaum S., Raynal M., and Stainer J., From wait-free to arbitrary concurrent solo executions in colorless distributed computing. *Theoretical Computer Science*, 683:1–21, 2017. DOI: 10.1016/j.tcs.2017.04.007 72

[74] Herlihy M. and Shavit N., *The Art of Multiprocessor Programming*. 508 pages, Morgan Kaufmann, 2008. 7

[75] Herlihy M. and Shavit N., The topological structure of asynchronous computability. *Journal of the ACM*, 46(6):858–923, 1999. DOI: 10.1145/331524.331529 25, 37, 43, 46, 54, 57, 59, 72, 73

[76] Herlihy M. P. and Wing J. M., Linearizability: A correctness condition for concurrent objects. *ACM Transactions on Programming Languages and Systems*, 12(3):463–492, 1990. DOI: 10.1145/78969.78972 5, 7, 33, 55

[77] Horowitz E. and Shani S., *Fundamentals of Computer Algorithms*. 626 pages, Pitman, 1978. 53

[78] Imbs D. and Raynal M., Visiting Gafni's reduction land: From the BG simulation to the extended BG simulation. *Proc. 11th International Symposium on Stabilization, Safety, and Security of Distributed Systems (SSS'09)*, pages 369–383, Springer LNCS 5873, 2009. DOI: 10.1007/978-3-642-05118-0_26 79

[79] Imbs D. and Raynal M., Help when needed, but no more: Efficient read/write partial snapshot. *Journal of Parallel and Distributed Computing*, 72(1):1–13, 2012. DOI: 10.1016/j.jpdc.2011.08.005 9

[80] Imbs D. and Raynal M., The multiplicative power of consensus numbers. *Proc. 29th ACM Symposium on Principles of Distributed Computing (PODC'10)*, pages 26–35, ACM Press, 2010. DOI: 10.1145/1835698.1835705 38

[81] Imbs D. and Raynal M., A liveness condition for concurrent objects: x-wait-freedom. *Concurrency and Computation: Practice and Experience*, 23:2154–2166, 2011. DOI: 10.1002/cpe.1741 8

[82] Imbs D. and Raynal M., Virtual world consistency: A condition for STM systems (with a versatile protocol with invisible read operations). *Theoretical Computer Science*, 444:113–127, 2012. DOI: 10.1016/j.tcs.2012.04.037 33, 88

[83] Imbs D. and Raynal M., Are Byzantine failures really different from crash failures? *Proc. 30th Symposium on Distributed Computing (DISC'16)*, pages 215–229, Springer LNCS 9888, 2016. DOI: 10.1007/978-3-662-53426-7_16 86

[84] Imbs D., Raynal M., and Taubenfeld G., On asymmetric progress conditions. *Proc. 29th ACM Symposium on Principles of Distributed Computing (PODC'10)*, pages 55–64, ACM Press, 2010. DOI: 10.1145/1835698.1835709 8, 41, 46

[85] Imbs D., Raynal M., and Taubenfeld G., Election in fully anonymous shared memory systems: Tight space bounds and algorithms. *Proc. 29th International Colloquium on Structural Information and Communication Complexity (SIROCCO'22)*, Springer LNCS, 2022. 97

[86] Inoue M., Chen W., Masuzawa T., and Tokura N., Linear time snapshot using multi-reader multi-writer registers. *Proc. 8th International Workshop on Distributed Algorithms (WDAG'94)*, pages 130–140, Springer LNCS 1857, 1994. DOI: 10.1007/bfb0020429 88

[87] Knuth D., *Selected Papers on Computer Science*, 274 pages, Cambridge University Press, 1996. 3

[88] Kramer S. N., *History Begins at Sumer: Thirty-Nine Firsts in Man's Recorded History*. 416 pages, University of Pennsylvania Press, 1956. 1

[89] Kuznetsov P., Universal model simulation: BG and extended BG as examples. *Proc. 15th International Symposium on Stabilization, Safety, and Security of Distributed Systems (SSS'13)*, pages 17–31, Springer LNCS 8255, 2013. DOI: 10.1007/978-3-319-03089-0_2 86

[90] Lamport L., Concurrent reading and writing. *Communications of the ACM*, 20(11):806–811, 1977. DOI: 10.1145/359863.359878 7

[91] Lamport L., Time, clocks, and the ordering of events in a distributed system. *Communications of the ACM*, 21(7):558–565, 1978. DOI: 10.1145/359545.359563 4, 23

[92] Lamport L., On interprocess communication, Part I: Basic formalism, Part II: Algorithms. *Distributed Computing*, 1(2):77–85, 1986. DOI: 10.1007/bf01786227 5, 55

[93] Lamport L., A fast mutual exclusion algorithm. *ACM Transactions on Computer Systems*, 5(1):1–11, 1987. DOI: 10.1145/7351.7352 19, 66

[94] Lamport L., *Specifying Systems*. 364 pages, Addison-Wesley, Pearson Education, 2003. 1

[95] Lamport L., Teaching concurrency. *ACM SIGACT NEWS*, 40(1):58–62, 2009. DOI: 10.1145/1515698.1515713 xxi

[96] Lamport L., Shostack R., and Pease M., The Byzantine generals problem. *ACM Transactions on Programming Languages and Systems*, 4(3):382–401, 982. DOI: 10.1145/357172.357176 4, 21, 53

[97] Loui M. and Abu-Amara H., Memory requirements for agreement among unreliable asynchronous processes. *Advances in Computing Research*, 4:163–183, JAI Press, 1987. 8, 35, 56, 73

[98] Lynch W. C., Computer Systems: Reliable full-duplex file transmission over half-duplex telephone line *Communications of the ACM*, 11(6):407–410, 1968. DOI: 10.1145/363347.363366 13

[99] Lynch N. A., *Distributed Algorithms*. 872 pages, Morgan Kaufmann Pub., San Francisco, CA, 1996. 54

[100] Mehlhorn K. and Sanders P., *Algorithms and Data Structures*. 300 pages, Springer, 2008. DOI: 10.1007/978-3-540-77978-0 53

[101] Moir M., Practical implementation of non-blocking synchronization primitives. *Proc. 16th ACM Symposium on Principles of Distributed Computing (PODC'97)*, pages 219–228, ACM Press, 1997. DOI: 10.1145/259380.259442 13

[102] Moret B., *The Theory of Computation*. 453 pages, Addison-Wesley, 1998. 3

[103] Mostéfaoui A., Perrin M., and Raynal M., A simple object that spans the whole consensus hierarchy. *Parallel Processing Letters*, 28(2), 9 pages, 2018. DOI: 10.1142/s0129626418500068 38

[104] Mostéfaoui A. Raynal M., and Travers C., Narrowing power vs. efficiency in synchronous set agreement: Relationship, algorithms, and lower bound. *Theoretical Computer Science* 411:58–69, 2010. DOI: 10.1016/j.tcs.2009.09.002 47

[105] Neugebauer O. E., *The Exact Sciences in Antiquity.* Princeton University Press, 1952; 2nd ed., Brown University Press, 1957; Reprint: Dover publications, 1969. 1

[106] Onofre J.-C., Rajsbaum S., and Raynal M., A topological perspective of recursion in distributed computing. *Technical Report*, 12 pages, UNAM, Mexico, 2013. 54, 55

[107] Pease M., Shostak R., and Lamport L., Reaching agreement in the presence of faults. *Journal of the ACM*, 27:228–234, 1980. DOI: 10.1145/322186.322188 36

[108] Perrin M., Mostéfaoui A., and Bonin G., Extending the wait-free hierarchy to multi-threaded systems. *Proc. 39th ACM Symposium on Principles of Distributed Computing (PODC'20)*, pages 21–30, ACM Press, 2020. DOI: 10.1145/3382734.3405723 41

[109] Peterson G. L., Concurrent reading while writing. *ACM Transactions on Programming Languages and Systems*, 5(1):46–55, 1983. DOI: 10.1145/357195.357198 7

[110] Post E. L., Formal reductions of the general combinatorial decision problem. *American Journal of Mathematics*, 65(2):197–215, 1943. DOI: 10.2307/2371809 3

[111] Rabin M. O. The choice coordination problem. *Acta Informatica*, 17:121–134, 1982. DOI: 10.1007/bf00288965 91

[112] Rachman O., Anomalies in the wait-free hierarchy. *Proc. 8th International Workshop on on Distributed Algorithms (WDAG'94, Now DISC Symposium)*, pages 156–163, Springer LNCS 857, 1994. DOI: 10.1007/bfb0020431 42, 51

[113] Rajsbaum S. and Raynal M., A theory-oriented introduction to wait-free synchronization based on the adaptive renaming problem. *Proc. 25th International Conference on Advanced Information Networking and Applications (AINA'11)*, pages 356–363, IEEE Press, 2011. DOI: 10.1109/aina.2011.9 64

[114] Rajsbaum S. and Raynal M., Mastering concurrent computing through sequential thinking: A half-century evolution. *Communications of the ACM*, 63(1):78–87, 2020. DOI: 10.1145/3363823 51

[115] Randell B., Recursively structured distributed computing systems. *Proc. 3rd Symposium on Reliability in Distributed Software and Database Systems*, pages 3–11, IEEE Press, 1983. 54

[116] Raynal M., *Concurrent Programming: Algorithms, Principles, and Foundations.* 515 pages, Springer, 2013. DOI: 10.1007/978-3-642-32027-9 xxi, 7, 9, 19, 23, 27, 36, 39, 56, 58, 61, 64, 67

[117] Raynal M., *Distributed Algorithms for Message-Passing Systems.* 515 pages, Springer, 2013. 4

[118] Raynal M., Concurrent systems: Hybrid object implementations and abortable objects. *Proc. 21th International European Parallel Computing Conference (EUROPAR'15)*, pages 3–15, Springer LNCS 9233, 2015. DOI: 10.1007/978-3-662-48096-0_1 19, 71

[119] Raynal M., Distributed universal constructions: A guided tour. *Electronic Bulletin of EATCS (European Association of Theoretical Computer Science)*, 121:65–96, 2017. 35, 50

[120] Raynal M., *Fault-Tolerant Message-Passing Distributed Systems: An Algorithmic Approach.* 492 pages, Springer, 2018. DOI: 10.1007/978-3-319-94141-7 xxi, 4, 38, 54

[121] Raynal M., The notion of universality in crash-prone asynchronous message-passing systems: A tutorial. *Proc. 38th International Symposium on Reliable Distributed Systems (SRDS 2019)*, 17 pages, IEEE Press, 2019. DOI: 10.1109/srds47363.2019.00046 xxi, 50

[122] Raynal M., Distributed computability: A few results masters students should know. *ACM SIGACT News, Distributed Computing Column*, 52(2):92–110, 2021. DOI: 10.1145/3471469.3471484 4

[123] Raynal M. and Stainer J., Simultaneous consensus vs. set agreement: A message-passing-sensitive hierarchy of agreement problems. *Proc. 20th International Colloquium on Structural Information and Communication Complexity (SIROCCO)*, pages 298–309, Springer LNCS 8179, 2013. DOI: 10.1007/978-3-319-03578-9_25 26

[124] Raynal M., Stainer J., and Taubenfeld G., Distributed universality. *Algorithmica*, 76(2):502–535, 2016. DOI: 10.1007/s00453-015-0053-3 31, 32

[125] Raynal M. and Taubenfeld G., Fully anonymous consensus and set agreement algorithms. *Proc. 8th International Conference on Networked Systems, (NETYS'20)*, pages 314–328, Springer LNCS 12129, 2020. DOI: 10.1007/978-3-030-67087-0_20 94, 95

[126] Raynal M. and Taubenfeld G., Mutual exclusion in fully anonymous shared memory systems. *Information Processing Letters*, 158(105938), 7 pages, 2020. DOI: 10.1016/j.ipl.2020.105938 97

[127] Roy M., BG distributed simulation algorithm. *Springer Encyclopedia of Algorithms*, 6 pages, 2015. DOI: 10.1007/978-3-642-27848-8_611-1 73

[128] Saks M. and Zaharoglou F., Wait-free *k*-set agreement is impossible: The topology of public knowledge. *SIAM Journal on Computing*, 29(5):1449–1483, 2000. DOI: 10.1137/s0097539796307698 25, 37, 43, 46, 72

[129] Schneider F. B., What good are models, and what models are good? *Distributed Systems*, 2nd ed., pages 17–26, Addison-Wesley/ACM Press, 1993. 1

[130] Shavit N. and Taubenfeld G., The computability of relaxed data structures: Queues and stacks as examples. *Distributed Computing*, 29(5):395–407, 2016. DOI: 10.1007/s00446-016-0272-0 39, 40

[131] Shavit N. and Touitou D., Software transactional memory. *Distributed Computing* 10(2):99–116, 1997. DOI: 10.1007/s004460050028 32

[132] Sipser M., *Introduction to the Theory of Computation*. 396 pages, PWS Publishing Company, 1996. 3

[133] Taubenfeld G., *Synchronization Algorithms and Concurrent Programming*. 423 pages, Pearson Education/Prentice Hall, 2006. 7, 9

[134] Taubenfeld G., Contention-sensitive data structure and algorithms. *Proc. 23rd International Symposium on Distributed Computing (DISC'09)*, pages 157–171, Springer LNCS 5805, 2009. DOI: 10.1007/978-3-642-04355-0_17 7, 9

[135] Taubenfeld G., Coordination without prior agreement. *Proc. 36th ACM Symposium on Principles of Distributed Computing (PODC'17)*, pages 325–334, ACM Press, 2017. DOI: 10.1145/3087801.3087807 91, 92

[136] Taubenfeld G., *Distributed Computing Pearls*. Synthesis Lectures on Distributed Computing Theory, Morgan & Claypool Publishers, 107 pages, 2018. DOI: 10.2200/S00845ED1V01Y201804DCT014 xxi

[137] Taubenfeld G., The set agreement power is not a precise characterization for oblivious deterministic anonymous objects. *Proc. 26th International Colloquium on Structural Information and Communication Complexity (SIROCCO'19)*, pages 290–304, Springer LNCS 11639, 2019. DOI: 10.1007/978-3-030-24922-9_20 51

[138] Taubenfeld G., The computational structure of progress conditions and shared objects. *Distributed Computing*, 33(2):103–123, 2020. DOI: 10.1007/s00446-019-00356-0 8, 40, 41

[139] Turing A. M., On computable numbers with an application to the Entscheidungsproblem. *Proc. of the London Mathematical Society*, 42:230–265, 1936. DOI: 10.1112/plms/s2-42.1.230 3

[140] Wantzel P. L., Recherches sur les moyens de reconnaître si un problème de géométrie peut se résoudre avec la règle et le compas, *Journal de Mathématiques Pures et Appliquées*, 1(2):366–372, 1837. 3

[141] Zhu L., A tight space bound for consensus. *Proc. 48th ACM Symposium on Theory of Computing (STOC'16)*, pages 345–350, ACM Press, 2016. DOI: 10.1145/2897518.2897565 33

Author's Biography

MICHEL RAYNAL

Michel Raynal is an Emeritus Professor of Informatics, IRISA, University of Rennes, France. He is an established authority in the domain of concurrent and distributed algorithms and systems. Author of numerous papers on this topic, Michel Raynal is a senior member of *Institut Universitaire de France*, and a member of Academia Europaea. He was the recipient of the 2015 *Innovation in Distributed Computing Award* (also known as SIROCCO Prize), recipient of the 2018 *IEEE Outstanding Technical Achievement in Distributed Computing Award*, and recipient of an *Outstanding Career Award* from the French chapter of ACM Sigops. He is also *Distinguished Chair Professor on Distributed Algorithms* at the Polytechnic University (PolyU) of Hong Kong.

Michel Raynal chaired the program committees of the major conferences on distributed computing. He was the recipient of several "Best Paper" awards of major conferences (including ICDCS 1999, 2000, and 2001, SSS 2009 and 2011, Europar 2010, DISC 2010, PODC 2014). He has also written 13 books on fault-tolerant concurrent and distributed systems, among which the following trilogy published by Springer: *Concurrent Programming: Algorithms: Principles and Foundations* (515 pages, 2013), *Distributed Algorithms for Message-passing Systems* (510 pages, 2013), and *Fault-Tolerant Message-Passing Distributed Systems: An Algorithmic Approach* (Springer, 459 pages, 2018).

Index

Printed in the United States
by Baker & Taylor Publisher Services